Back in the Garden Again

Back in the Garden Again

The Mystery Hidden for Ages, and Now Revealed to Us

Graeme Schultz

Gobsmacked Publishing

All Scripture quotations, unless otherwise indicated, are taken from the Holy Bible, New International Version®, NIV®. Copyright ©1973, 1978, 1984, 2011 by Biblica, Inc.™ Used by permission of Zondervan. All rights reserved worldwide. www.zondervan.com The "NIV" and "New International Version" are trademarks registered in the United States Patent and Trademark Office by Biblica, Inc.™

Copyright © 2016 by Graeme Schultz.
All rights reserved. No part of this publication may be reproduced, distributed or transmitted in any form or by any means, including photocopying, recording, or other electronic or mechanical methods, without the prior written permission of the publisher, except in the case of brief quotations embodied in critical reviews and certain other noncommercial uses permitted by copyright law. For permission requests, write to the publisher, addressed "Permissions Coordinator," at the address below.

Graeme Schultz/Gobsmacked Publishing
19 Trotters Lane,
Cudgee, Victoria, Australia, 3265.
www.gobsmackedpublishing.com.au

National Library of Australia Cataloguing-in-Publication Entry
Creator: Schultz, Graeme, author.
Title: Back in the garden again : the mystery hidden for ages, and now revealed to us / Graeme Schultz.
ISBN: 9780994603005 (paperback)

Subjects: Christian life.
Spiritual life–Christianity.
God–Knowableness.
God–Love.
Dewey Number: 248.4

Dedicated to Angela

Preface

My intention in writing this book has been to show that there is a way to be a Christian that most of us have never experienced or thought possible. Adam and Eve lived a life of wonder and intimacy with God before there was sin - it is this same life that Christ came to give us back again.

The way to this life is a narrow, less crowded road - and few find it. Yet it awaits us all.

I have deliberately written in a way that is more conversational than instructional. My intention in this conversation is not to tell you how to think or believe; only you can do that. Rather, I have described an alternative way to think as a Christian.

Paul called it 'The Mystery Hidden for Ages'.

Contents

Introduction.	1
Chapter 1. The Human Drama	5
Chapter 2. Creation & Re-Creation	9
Chapter 3. What Went Wrong?	15
Chapter 4. Enlightenment	21
Chapter 5. Flesh Deeds Spirit Deeds	25
Chapter 6. Feeding on Christ	31
Chapter 7. The Pearl of Great Price	37
Chapter 8. Seeing and Knowing	45
Chapter 9. The Old Nature	51
Chapter 10. The New Nature	55
Chapter 11. The Big 10	59
Chapter 12. The Covenants	63
Chapter 13. Why Are We Here?	67
Chapter 14. Letting Go	71
Chapter 15. How to Receive	77
Chapter 16. The Body of Christ	83
Chapter 17. Beyond Grace	87
Chapter 18. To See The Invisible	93

Chapter 19. Who Can Come?	97
Chapter 20. Eternity	101
Chapter 21. Christ in Me	105
Chapter 22. Empty That We May Be Filled	109
Conclusion	113

Introduction.

I'VE been a Christian for a long time, pretty much my whole life.

I know my way around the place - the language, the system, and the culture have been second nature to me for as long as I can remember. It has been my stomping ground, the place where I fit-in.

A few years back I had to make a serious admission to myself – it wasn't working!

It was a major crisis in my business activities which proved to me that it wasn't working. The Global Financial Crisis hit hard, and I lost a life's work. All the spiritual language, all the systemized programs, and all of the activities of the culture gave me no answers, the great big machine we call Christianity didn't come through for me. Sure, there were lots of pious platitudes and spiritual rhetoric – but in the end they were simply the repeated party lines of a system that didn't deliver.

I made up my mind that I wouldn't settle for that kind of Christianity anymore.

I decided to discover a deeper way; a way that didn't depend on the busy activities and worn-out clichés. A way that was less about the system, and more about the God we named the system after.

This book is about that discovery.

This discovery had its beginning in a perfect world where God could be counted upon with absolute certainty, then something went wrong – and we (the human race) lost our way. Then Jesus carried us back to that place of certainty, where it all began.

The problem for me was that I didn't understand what it actually was that Jesus had done... *and unfortunately for me, the church system didn't seem to either.* I understood a lot of things on a cerebral level, but they were a part of the broad information bank of Christianity – rather than a deep revelation of Jesus himself.

It takes a lot of re-thinking, and not a small amount of courage, to critically examine the thing that has been your stomping ground for life – but it's been so very worth it!

Here's how it happened...

For the greater part of my life I considered the narrative about the Garden of Eden *(contained in the first three chapters of Genesis)* as simply an intro into a much bigger story. It was a useful snap-shot of the beginning that would set the scene for the real story that followed. The story of humanity; the good, the bad and the ugly... *our story.* The drama of mankind, and God, and life on planet earth - thousands of years of history rolled into one long, epic adventure.

Now I'm not so sure.

Now I think the real story was captured in those first three chapters; and the narrative that followed, *epic as it was,* was simply the drama of humanity's long road back home to the garden.

A garden that contains within it, the natural realm of the Garden of Eden (as described in Genesis), but also vastly more than this natural context. It is the greater garden of the spiritual realm, the Garden of God, or Paradise, the garden of God's pleasure. This realm of the Spirit was as real before time began, as it will be when Christ returns in glory. And it was a place as relevant to Adam and Eve, as it is to us today, and in eternity.

For me this was a critical difference.

It seemed that as long as I remained captivated by the epic adventure of humanity, played out on the stage of nature, I was unable to see the grander view that lay behind the human story. A bit like thinking the 'Punch and Judy show' is the real thing - when in fact it is merely the visible drama on show before our eyes.

This grander view, *this garden narrative,* has brought a new order to my somewhat disconnected, narrow view of things. My eyes have begun to view a landscape vastly broader than before. My earlier thinking was constrained within the safe harbor of well-crafted, earth-based, human reasoning. I have lifted anchor, and departed safe waters, for the adventure of Life in the Spirit. At last I can truly say that my faith in God makes sense, at last I am at peace with myself, with God, and with life.

That's a big statement to make.

For the greater part of my life (before this discovery), I would have considered such a statement to be unrealistic and even presumptuous. Now I am relieved to experience as normal, what previously had seemed so elusive and unreachable.

I will do my best to unpack this discovery over the pages and chapters that follow. I hope in spite of my unsophisticated words, and ineloquent language, you will see through to a mystery so vast that you too will sit stunned by the magnificence of a salvation so great. This mysterious salvation was enacted by a God who is way beyond our human reasoning, and systemized cultural thinking – yet he has made his home in us.

Chapter 1.
The Human Drama

THERE was a time when I was quite content with what I will term 'the Human Drama' as a platform upon which I could construct my life. This *man-made* system of the visible realm, held all the ingredients I considered necessary to construct a proper way to live; right principles, decent behavior, good habits, religious lifestyle. All combined to make up a life that would please God, and put me in good stead with my neighbor.

In reality the opposite unfolded. My financial security unraveled before my eyes, and a life's work was lost in a few short years. I was at the end of my self. I had done all I could do. I had dug deep and called forth every last fiber of my natural ability – but it wasn't enough, and I stood back and watched it all go down the drain.

It's not particularly relevant that it was my life's material work that was lost - it could have been anything - health, marriage, loss of any kind… *whatever!*

> *The important thing is that I came to the end of myself.*
> *I ran out of options, and so I began to examine the platform upon*
> *which my life was built.*

I mean, really examine it… I was ready to walk away from the faith I had known my whole life - I was ready to say that it had all been a waste of time.

So I had one last conversation with God (a God who I wasn't even convinced existed)… I said; "God, I am running on empty. I don't think I can believe in you anymore; please show me Jesus, I simply can't go on this way any longer".

From this one question has emerged a faith I didn't think possible.

The 'Human Drama' mindset that had been my beacon for so many years was built deeply into my nature. I wasn't particularly conscious of it, nor did I deliberately call it into action. It was simply who I was. It was the subconscious operating system… *that was programmed in to me.*

It functioned something like this: "Good things happen to good people, so I had better be as good as I can be". If I live right, if I honor God with my life, if I treat humanity with kindness and decency – then I can expect favor and blessing in return. I guess you could call it a Christian 'karma' – *you get what you give…* "God can't shower you with his best if you don't keep your end up".

The 'Human Drama' came into play when it's predecessor 'Life in the Spirit' was abandoned by Adam and Eve. They chose a new operating system for humanity; one based on man's best, not God's. This system has been in operation for thousands of years now; the 'Human Drama' is set in stone - it is the operating system of humanity. The arrival of Christ, his life, and subsequent death for the forgiveness of our sins, has been interpreted by the masses as reinforcing this operating system. *Christ provided the best model of a life well lived; and now we have a real example to follow – all we have to do is walk in his footsteps.*

But how wrong we have been to view Christ's work through the lens of the 'Human Drama'.

The 'Human Drama' is humanity constructing its identity from what it does, instead of from its union with God. It is the epic drama of human history played out on the stage of the natural world. The players were created as spiritually-alive beings, but they opted-out in favor of a completely natural existence.

The 'Human Drama' is a term I have quoined; others have used different terminology. Jesus called it 'the Flesh' in John 6:63. Paul called it 'the Sinful Nature' in Rom. 7:18 & Gal. 5:24. I have quoined this new term because we seem to have rationalized 'the Flesh' and 'the Sinful Nature' as the bad part of our human existence. The flesh (or sinful nature) is so much more than the sum total of our worst days. Even our best days are devoid of value (mere filthy rags) - if we look to ourselves for our sense of worth.

It seems we have decided that our behavior or lifestyle is the measure of whether we are, or are not, living in the flesh, or the spirit. *The reality is that our behavior may be the worst measure of all.*

The realm of nature is the stage where we are most visible; but there is another stage, an invisible one, where our spirits are at home with God – this is where the true reality is found.

What I am saying is that our compulsion to live according to the rules of the 'Human Drama', and to measure our worth according to our determination to live right here on planet earth, is the very thing that is keeping us from the thing we want most – Life in the Spirit.

> ***It is keeping us from Life in the Spirit,***
> ***because the Spirit is not fuelled by human effort,***
> ***but by the life-giving nature of Christ.***

The laws that govern the 'Human Drama' are simply this; "My best behavior, my noblest actions, and my most fervent Christian lifestyle, are the elements that cause God to be pleased with me, and consequently to release his flow of blessing and favor into my life"… *positioning me for a spiritual life.*

Even as I write this I know many will agree with that last sentence. We agree with it because it is ingrained into our nature – *it's our operating system* – and we truly believe that it is what God wants.

We believe it's how he planned things all along.

It seems to be our conviction that God is scrutinizing our lives in the hope of finding 'right living' – (and that is the most sinister of all satan's lies). In fact, it is the very thing that caused all the trouble in the Garden of Eden in the first place, and has held man captive ever since (even in the church). The reason that this deception is so sinister is that it seems so right. It seems both reasonable and logical that God would be primarily concerned with the way we live our lives – and so, we miss the better, more excellent way… *'Life in the Spirit'*.

In reality, God is scrutinizing our lives to find faith in the person and work of Jesus… *period!*

Strangely, this 'Life in the Spirit' has little to do with good behavior (even though good behavior follows as the overflow) – it is hardly conscious of 'getting it right' at all. Rather, it is consumed with the righteousness of Christ, which has made its home in the believer, and has become the power house for a life well lived.

Don't get me wrong, I value a respectable and generous life as much as the next person – but it is not this personal behavior that gains our access to the heart of God, it is faith in the precious blood of Jesus.

There is much to cover in explaining this matter of 'Right Living' v. 'Life in the Spirit' – and we will get to it… but for now let's return to the garden, and look again at those first three chapters afresh.

Chapter 2.
Creation & Re-Creation

I am convinced that the reason Christ came, was to restore humanity back to 'Life in the Garden of God'. Or take it a step further – 'Life in the Garden' and 'Life in the Spirit' are exactly the same thing.

I grew up with the impression that Adam's existence in the garden was relatively independent of God.

Sure they would catch up for a chat in the cool of the evening, and God certainly had a watchful eye on his creation, but by-and-large Adam's world and God's world didn't overlap much. Adam did his thing, and God did his thing, and they caught up to share on a regular basis as all good friends do.

It wasn't so much that God was keeping his distance or didn't care… its more that God had got the whole thing started, and so he stood back and let Adam (and Eve) get on with being in charge of the best garden ever. I guess you could say; God had created the most stunning world imaginable, and when it was finished he rested and settled back into heaven to see how things played out. Christ and the Holy Spirit were not particularly present, other than their default positions as members of the trinity.

I don't see things that way anymore.

In the past I didn't see any connection between the perfect <u>creation</u> that God made simply by speaking the **Word**, and the perfect <u>re-creation</u> that God made when he sent the **Living Word** - Jesus.

I thought they were two relatively unrelated events in history – one at the start of the Old Testament, and one at the start of the New Testament. The creation story in Genesis 1-3 was the story of man's beginning, and the salvation story in the 4 gospels was man's forgiveness for his rebellion against God. They were separate matters, and were nothing more than 2 periods in the history of human kind - both of which involved man's sin, but had little else in common.

The link between these two periods in human history is 'The Tree of the Knowledge of Good and Evil'. Adam was created to feed on 'The Tree of Life' forever – but he opted out of God's provision of life, and chose an existence for humanity independent of God. This self-based existence is a daily diet of 'The Tree of The Knowledge of Good and Evil' – it has been humanities dining table for thousands of years.

'The Tree of the Knowledge of Good and Evil' is the choice to draw our sustenance and identity from what we do, instead of from the life God gives.

It is all about us; how well we juggle the 'good v. evil' equation.

Now that I have made the connection between these two periods in history, I am convinced that Adam's pre-sin existence in the Garden of Eden - is exactly the same as our existence in Christ today. God has given us back the old diet plan that Adam started with.

In effect, by believing in Jesus we have returned to the Garden of God. Adam's inherent worth and perfection (which was his daily experience as a man created by God in his own image), is the very same as ours now. Just as Adam was born of God, we are re-born of God - (John 1:13). God's perfect creation was sabotaged by Adam, and has been re-made by Christ.

Let's consider what Adam and Eve's existence was like before sin entered in.

Adam was made in God's image – *what exactly does that mean?*

Chapter 2. Creation & Re-Creation

Could it be that Adam was created out of the same ingredients as God? Righteousness, holiness, goodness!

Adam was not God (capital 'G') but he was born out of God. He had the body and soul of a man, and he had a spirit in perfect union with God. He had the same perfect nature as God. There was absolutely no difference between God's nature and Adam's nature - they had identical divine-natured hearts.

It's interesting that 2 Peter 1:4 says we are participating in the 'Divine Nature', John 1:13 says that we are 'Born of God', and Hebrews 10:14 says we have been 'Made perfect'. I had previously read these scriptures as somewhat loose terms used in a very general way. Now I see that they are very specific, that they apply to me and all believers, and they are the absolute fact upon which our lives are founded.

The logical conclusion is this;
"Just as Adam shared the identical nature of God, so also do I".

Simply by placing faith in the life-giving work of Christ I am translated from my old sinful nature - to my new divine nature. It is not something I do, or a process that I am in as I mature in my lifestyle. It is a fact completed in its entirety in a twinkling of an eye... just by believing in Jesus.

Just as Adam could not have 2 natures neither can I.

There is no tension, or fight for supremacy within me, as 2 natures wrestle for the upper hand. Rather, I am now a God-natured man – and satan's only work is to attempt to deceive me into thinking that I need to add my good works to Christ's - to be truly pleasing to God.

He wants me living life in the 'Human Drama' - and he wants to keep me out of the Garden where I belong.

As long as he can keep me focused on my own efforts I will never step boldly into my new God-born nature, and assume my God-given righteous status.

Satan knows that I have been re-created back into the image of God, he knows that I am seated with Christ in heaven, he knows that I am a perfect God-natured man… *he is simply determined to keep me from knowing it.*

It is what he does; he is the father of lies.

I had always assumed that my salvation status was inferior to Adam's pre-sin life. I thought that Adam had a clean slate - whereas I had a slate covered by sins (sins which were crossed out by Jesus).

Adam was pure, whereas I was forgiven.

This thinking kept me on the Human Drama bandwagon. It kept me trying to find my identity in what I do – instead of in my union with Christ. I didn't understand that Adam's pure state, and my forgiven state, were exactly the same. So this thinking kept me attempting to attain a life of purity that was reflective of my forgiven state, my life was focused on my own acts of righteousness - instead of resting in Christ's gift of righteousness.

Getting back to Life in the Garden; my old view of Adam's relative independence from God seemed to be at odds with discoveries I was making in the New Testament. I was reading such scriptures as Gal. 2:20 'Christ lives in me', Col. 3:3 'Your life is hidden with Christ in God', John 14:20 'I am in my Father, and you are in me, and I am in you'. These scriptures speak of the re-born union with God, which I received from Christ. Adam didn't need to be re-born, he was the original made in God's image - and I am simply a later version of the same.

So I have concluded that the union with God that the New Testament assigned to me simply by believing in Jesus - is the very same union that Adam enjoyed.

Chapter 2. Creation & Re-Creation

Adam and I share exactly the same union with God.

According to John 14:20, it's also the union that Jesus enjoyed when he walked the earth. Jesus was able to view this union in all its wonder and glory because the sinful nature was not obstructing his view; similarly Adam was also fully aware of this union, before sin obstructed his view.

This 'Union' that Adam enjoyed at first, was a union that has been unknown to humankind between the time of the fall into sin, until the redemptive work of Christ. There has been no comparison for us to guide our thinking, no counterpart in the realm of human relations. This union is unique; it is the sharing of one divine nature between two individuals. Adam lived within this union for every moment of every day; it was the life source of his existence. He was physically nourished by food and drink to keep his body alive, and he was spiritually nourished by his union with God to keep his spirit alive.

In that regard; Adam was primarily a spiritual man living in a natural environment - rather than a natural man who touched the spiritual realm from time to time.

The Tree of Life gave him this spiritual nourishment continually.

It's interesting to read the references to 'Life' as it pertains to Jesus from the book of John.

John 1:4 - 'In him was Life'.

John 5:26 - 'For as the Father has Life in himself, so he has granted the Son to have Life in himself'.

John 10:10 - 'I came that they might have Life'.

John 14:6 - 'I am the way, the truth and the Life'.

Jesus not only had Life, he was Life.

It's reasonable to join the dots and conclude that Jesus' role throughout the ages has been to give Life. He is the source that maintains our spirit in its living vitality, without his life our spirit is dead to God. The Father granted Life to Jesus, (John 5:26) and Jesus gives Life to us. It is a flow of the divine nature constantly filling us - just because we are 'in Christ'.

I wonder if Adam was nourished spiritually by Jesus just as we are. I wonder if the flow of Life that kept his spirit vitally alive was in fact Jesus himself. Jesus speaks of us feeding on him in John 6:46 – "so the one who feeds on me will live because of me". Perhaps Adam fed on Jesus just as we do, and in the context of Eden, Jesus and the Tree of Life were synonymous.

We read in Ezekiel 31 the descriptive way that Egypt is compared to a tree in Eden, the garden of God… If a nation can be likened to a tree, it is reasonable to conclude that Jesus can also be likened to a tree – The Tree of Life.

I say all of this in an attempt to paint a picture of life in the garden, *a different narrative if you like.* This narrative views the Genesis story from the realm of the Spirit, rather than the realm of the earth. It is a picture that has as its focus an essentially spiritual existence between Adam and Eve (in their union with God), as opposed to a natural existence within an earthly environment. This existence was entirely comfortable within the reality of the spiritual realm, while living in a natural body that functioned through its five senses and intellect. You could say that; "Though they were in the world, they were not of the world".

It's an important distinction because it clearly defines 'what went wrong' and how life changed as a result of Adam and Eve's rebellion.

Chapter 3.
What Went Wrong?

My earlier view of Adam & Eve as essentially natural people (prior to their fall into sin) had formed a picture in my mind of 'what went wrong' and consequently 'what followed'.

Natural people do natural things, make natural mistakes, and natural consequences result. On the other hand, if they were fully fledged spiritual people then their rebellious actions were entirely different - and so were the consequences.

This begs the question, "What exactly did they do wrong?"

If we read the Genesis story from a purely natural standpoint, then Adam & Eve were disobedient. God commanded them not to eat from the Tree of the Knowledge of Good & Evil, and their sin was a straightforward matter of yielding to satan's temptation, and disobeying God. God had provided just one rule - *and they broke it.*

If, on the other hand, we read the Genesis story from a spiritual standpoint, then Adam & Eve's problem was not disobedience but independence. As spiritual people they had a clear understanding of the flow of virtue, and worth, which was their daily fare from God. This was a filling of spiritual life as they fed on their union with God. They knew that righteousness and holiness were provided to them continually - simply by feeding on the Tree of

Life. They had no awareness of Good & Evil because their nature was perfect in every way.

You might be thinking, "How can perfect people sin?"

> *The answer is that they can't sin while they have a perfect nature – they can however choose to be independent of that nature.*

It was the choice to be independent of God that resulted in the loss of their perfect nature. The effect of having a godless nature is that one must generate from within, the righteousness required to live well, and it also opens the way for sin. This existence is constantly negotiating the 'Good & Evil equation' to secure the happiness, well-being, and security, that humankind thrives upon. It is a behavior-based existence, where reward, punishment, and acceptance, are purchased by the buying power of our right / or wrong living.

At its most basic level, the temptation satan waved before Adam & Eve was vanity. Like satan, they were magnificent creations of the Most High God, created in his spitting image. All satan needed to do was turn their attention to themselves and he had them. All he had to do was sow the seed of self-based worth, instead of God-given worth. His deception was far more sinister than disobedience; it was that he lured them into his own thinking… "*They could be god for themselves*".

It had always seemed unrealistic to me that Adam & Eve had suffered so much, for such a minor infringement. Surely picking forbidden fruit and eating it, was not sufficient cause for God to throw them, and the entire human race, out of the garden – *especially if God is so loving and just!* Banishment of this sort would involve a far more significant error than simply a bad choice in fruit picking. Banishment would involve a quantum failure, not a misdemeanor.

> *This sort of banishment would involve a personal choice to live independent of God.*

Chapter 3. What Went Wrong?

Did Adam & Eve fully grasp what they were getting themselves into? – *Probably not.* Yet the temptation to construct a life based on their own merits, their own wisdom, their own view of things, was too much – *they were hooked.*

Indeed they did begin a life that responded to their juggling of Good & Evil. They did gain a worldly wisdom beyond their previous holy naivety, and they did see for the first time that life's circumstances produce new challenges and opportunities. But all of these came at a great cost… *they couldn't fellowship with God on the same basis as before.*

They were out-casts - now living in a realm that judged their daily lives.

The normal outcome of 'criminal behavior' in the world system would involve punishment perhaps, and for a serious matter, even jail time. In any event the judicial system would mete out a punitive response as fits the crime. Our natural inclination is to fit the failings of Adam & Eve into the judicial environment of the world we live in - *to apportion a form of penalty for wrongs done.*

As a result we take such scriptures as "the wages of sin is death" to be the meeting out of punishment by a righteously judgmental God. In other words – *God is the one applying the judicial response.* He has a standard that we have broken, and we must pay for our failure to live up to his standard.

When we view the failings of Adam & Eve from the spiritual realm we see quite the opposite. We see a God who daily provides righteousness to us for free. Good & evil are not even on the screen; just an unrelenting flow of virtue from God's never ending supply of goodness and mercy.

It stands to reason therefore, that this judicial response is not coming from the Kingdom of God, but from another location where such a response is normal. I can only conclude that this judgmental environment is the currency of the 'kingdom of darkness', and it is applied to humankind because Adam & Eve made it their home.

They handed satan the legal basis to be judged by their actions – it was all part of taking control of their destiny and choosing to generate their own righteousness, rather than receiving it for free from Christ.

Accordingly, Adam and Eve (and the whole human race) are not under punishment from God.

Rather they are under the punishment-based regime of an alternative system. It is a system that judges their lives, and penalizes accordingly. God is not connected to this system; it is entirely the making of man's self-based way of thinking. Man has constructed a system of self-worthiness that operates entirely apart from God. It's not so much that God is punishing man for getting it wrong; it's that man has chosen a pathway independent from the workings of God's kingdom.

Ultimately God would have to step into man's system to resolve things; we will discuss that soon – but for now the thing to grasp is that God is not directing this system - man is directing it *by default.*

The importance of this distinction can't be understated. In fact it is the reason that the church and many Christians continue to operate according to the rules of the 'Human Drama'. If we think that Christ came to merely pay a penalty, we will remain locked in a *'reward / punishment for behavior'* focused mindset. This link between disobedience, and the resulting consequences, is deeply ingrained because it has shaped humanity for millennia; in fact it is the way of the natural realm.

If we were still people of the natural realm we would continue to be subject to the demanding code which defines the 'Human drama', to maintain our worth. But we have been translated out of that realm back to the garden. It is a garden where our spirits are vitally alive, and the nourishment of Christ's righteous life is ours again for free.

> *Tragically, many remain trapped in the natural realm through lack of knowledge.*

Chapter 3. What Went Wrong?

Christ did not come to merely pay our penalty (amazing as that would be alone), he came to crucify our 'Dead to God' spirit and re-birth it with his own.

Christ came onto the human stage to accomplish this, yet his deepest work was not in the natural realm. The natural realm simply gave him access to the kingdom of darkness so that he could confront satan as the second Adam. He was a man in every way – yet not one living according to the 'Human drama'; he confronted him as a man who had the nature of God.

The divine nature of Christ enabled him to live on a plain above the expectations of the world system. He could heal on the Sabbath, he could curse a fig tree, he could turn water into gallons of wine – all because he didn't have a good v. evil mentality. Instead he had the righteous nature of God which operated spontaneously outside of the carefully-crafted protocols of man's system. His Spirit lived in the Garden of God's love - a place without the limits of human expectation. His actions were generated by a force far superior to the man-made model. His actions were the overflow of the union between him and his Father; you could say they were God's actions – *he just naturally walked in the Spirit.*

It is this alternative way that has failed to take hold in much of the Christian culture today. People are told Sunday after Sunday that they are still required to function according to the rules of the 'Human Drama' - *as if our true existence is still of this earth.* We are taught Sunday after Sunday how to live right, when all along the Spirit is telling us that Christ lived right for us.

Subtly our hearts hear the same lie that satan told in the first place, "You are the sum of your best deeds".

It is a vicious cycle; an inescapable treadmill. The only way out is to caste ourselves off the treadmill, and into Christ. And the only way to do that is to completely lift our eyes off ourselves for our sense of worth, and onto Christ… (who is our righteousness).

Knowing how amazing the salvation is that was provided to us by Christ, you would assume that all Christians would immediately step off the treadmill of the 'Human Drama' and into the restful existence called 'Life in the Spirit'.

But, by and large we don't – *go figure!*

Chapter 4.
Enlightenment

THE Apostle Paul articulated this dilemma in the epistles to the Romans and Ephesians.

He begins the book of Romans praising the Roman believers in chapter 1, verse 8, "First, I thank my God through Jesus Christ for all of you, because your faith is being reported all over the world". Clearly they were a vibrant, faith filled Christian community. Yet in Romans 12:2 he exhorts them "Do not conform any longer to the pattern of this world but be transformed by the renewing of your mind". On the one hand he recognizes them as people of faith, yet informs them that their minds are holding them back – a transformation beyond their present condition awaits, if they will sort out their thinking.

Similarly, in the book of Ephesians; he raises no doctrinal issues, he addresses no moral behavior, and he has no correction for them. Yet, he prays in chapter 1, verse 18, "That the eyes of their heart may be enlightened in order that they may know the hope to which they have been called, the riches of their inheritance, and God's incomparably great power for them". On the one hand they are a community that requires no particular correction, yet Paul identifies that the vastness of their salvation has still not registered in their hearts.

These 2 examples illustrate the problem that besets humanity. We receive the message of Christ unto salvation, yet our thinking (or enlightenment of hearts) does not automatically follow. And so we live out a form of Christianity that is only half formed at best, and in many cases having little grasp of the scale of the thing that we are in. And it is all because we have not brought our thinking into line with the bigger reality.

We are saved: *but we don't know how to live the saved life!*

On one level it is an appalling waste of Christ's blood that he could have provided so much, yet we barely scratch the surface in terms of our revelation of what we have. Yet on the other hand it is not surprising that we have such a meager grasp of our salvation, when our thinking remains stuck in the tracks of post-Eden history.

Paul celebrated that these communities of believers were bound for heaven, he applauded their faithfulness and service – yet he declared loud and clear, "There is more!" The words 'transformation' and 'enlightenment' can't be swept under the carpet. Paul puts them out there for a reason - not to diminish the believer's experience of God so far, but to inform them that their understanding is limiting the scale of their experience.

As far as our salvation is concerned, it is a 'given'. We see the kindness of God expressed through the person and work of Christ, and we say "Yes!" Call it repentance, call it revelation, whatever! It becomes ours because we see it, and receive it – *God's gift for the taking.*

Yet the rest of our inheritance is not so easily apprehended. It seems that we enter eternal life with relative ease, but then spend the rest of our days figuring out how to make it work.

It seems to me that the problem lays in our minds and our sight. The reason is that we retain the minds and sight of the 'Human Drama' or Old Nature. We were supposed to bring our minds into agreement with the wonders of salvation gifted to us by Jesus - but instead we apply the very thinking that expelled man from Eden in the first place, as we attempt to live saved.

Chapter 4. Enlightenment

We take the wonder of <u>pre-sin</u> Eden, and attempt to lay hold of it with <u>post-sin</u> thinking.

The defining difference between post-sin and pre-sin thinking, is the notion that man derives his worth from the good & evil he commits, rather than from Christ. In other words; our deeds validate us v. our union with Christ validates us. Or yet another way to put it; we continue to eat from the Tree of the Knowledge of Good and Evil, even though we have been welcomed back to the Garden and provided with the Tree of Life.

Perhaps the most troubling of all is that the majority of Christians, in the majority of churches around the world, are doing it. They have received salvation as a gift, and then set about crafting a life out of 'human drama thinking' that contradicts the very essence of Christ's gift. Jesus himself went so far as to say in John 6:63 "The Spirit gives life; the flesh counts for nothing". Yet we re-elevate the deeds of the flesh to spiritual status because our un-renewed minds don't know the difference.

Paul was scathing of the Galatian church in chapter 3 according to his famous 'You foolish Galatians' tirade. Strangely; he was not strongly critical of any moral or lifestyle matter - but he said that they were bewitched into thinking they could receive the Spirit by believing, only to try and attain it by human effort.

Similarly; most Christians I know are more concerned with a squeaky-clean lifestyle, than a believing-based walk in the Spirit. It seems to be our default position – we have re-packaged 'works of the flesh' and called them 'works of the spirit', because we cannot see, or understand, the alternative.

If you are still with me I congratulate you – this can be challenging stuff (and perhaps all the more challenging because of my stammering words).

At this point many people cry out "But that would give people a license to sin". Fact is: people are sinning both within, and out, of the church without a license. Sin is not just what we do, it is who we are – it is our post-Eden nature. The only way to really address sin is to grasp 'Living in the Spirit' – the flesh has nothing to contribute here, (it is our fallen nature) – we must take the risk of walking away from it and learn to rest and rely entirely on the Spirit.

Blending the flesh and the spirit doesn't work either. Mixing Christ's work with our own good deeds is a watered down cocktail that lacks any kick at all. The only way is to rest in Christ's work period – *all of him and none of me*. Then finally the Spirit can commence the deeds prepared for us before the beginning of time - *this is 'Living in the Spirit'*.

The inclination of our Old Nature is to get a balance between Christ's work and ours. In reality this is the lie satan wants us to believe. There is no balance... *it is one or the other.*

Even though we have been re-created back into the image of God – our natural inclination is to attempt to create God to be more like our own image. We want him to provide us with a salvation that validates our Old Nature and its compulsion to find worth in its own deeds. We want God to value the very thing that caused us to break away from him in the Garden – our decision to be our own life-source, instead of him.

I will spend the next chapter working through the difference between flesh deeds and Spirit deeds – it takes quite a bit of re-thinking, so stay with me.

Chapter 5.
Flesh Deeds
Spirit Deeds

It's fair to say that the majority of Christians want to walk in the Spirit. It is my observation, and past personal experience also, that it is probably the most elusive of all Christian endeavors. To a large extent this is because the deeds of the flesh, and the deeds of the Spirit, can appear to be exactly the same.

Indeed I doubt many people actually think there is any difference. As long as we are doing things that have a connection to Christianity at large, most people would regard their activities as spiritually valid.

It can come as quite a shock to well-intentioned Christians, when they learn that their activities are no more spiritual, than the activities of the pagan down the street. Paul made a statement that is so radical it blows away all of our previous notions of the value of much of what we do; Romans 14:23 says "whatever is not from faith is sin".

Strong words! Why would he say such a thing? Much of my Christian activity contains little application of faith… does that make it sin? That would mean I really am no more spiritual than the pagan down the street.

I believe the point Paul is making is not that we have to be deeply applying deliberate faith to all of our Christian activities – but rather that we must grasp that true faith rests in who we are, not what we do. It rests in a deep understanding that we been re-birthed with the nature of God.

And I guess that's the nub of it; the Tree of the Knowledge of Good and Evil gave humanity a 'doing' focused nature - in place of the 'being' focused nature that came from the Tree of Life. Jesus told people to abide in him, but to a large extent we find that very hard to do – and so instead we settle for mere Christian activity.

True faith is a state of mind (a revelation of Christ in me), not an activity that we apply ourselves to. It is a place of rest, that we can do all things in Christ – *not in ourselves*.

Most churches I know direct the flock to; get serious, get committed, and get on with the work of the kingdom. It is the same mantra that the world listens to – go for it, just do it, etc. It is nothing more than carnal thinking masquerading as spirituality. True spirituality has little to say about what we do, and much to say about what Christ did – *and who we are as a result.* When we see him as he is we become like him, and works of life flow spontaneously from us like rivers of living water.

> ***True spirituality has little to say about what we do,
> and much to say about what Christ did
> – and who we are as a result.***

We don't need to turn-on our good works – we need to fix our eyes on Jesus, from whom all good things come. Having fixed our eyes on him, and grasped the magnitude of our salvation, works of the spirit bubble up like a fountain... *rather than being forced out like a pump.*

Perhaps the most scandalous statement I will make in this book is that *"God doesn't care what you do"* – but he cares a great deal that you gain a revelation of what Christ has done... *stay with me now.*

Chapter 5. Flesh Deeds Spirit Deeds

It is scandalous because it has the potential to bring the whole house of cards tumbling down (and we wouldn't want that). If people stopped doing the stuff Christians do, then who would feed the hungry, who would preach to the lost, and who would pray for the sick? These are compelling questions indeed, they can't be sweep aside.

Yet surprisingly, they have the potential to distract us from the superior way of the Spirit.

I wonder how it worked back in the garden. It wasn't until Adam was cast out of the garden that he had to produce food by the sweat of his brow. The implication is that there was a better way to get one's food supply before the 'fall'. And if there was a better way to get one's food supply, perhaps there was a better way to get everything else done - a kind of labor that was restful and leaned into God's strength not our own.

Paul had it figured out in Colossians 1:29 "To this end I strenuously contend with all the energy Christ so powerfully works in me" And again in Ephesians 1:19 "and his incomparably great power for us who believe. That power is the same as the mighty strength, which he exerted in Christ when he raised him from the dead".

It is not ceasing from our labors, but a different kind of labor that has God as its powerhouse… *not us*.

This labor is altogether different from any labor known to man since he resided in Eden. And it is the only labor that produces the Life that Christ came to give, in John 10:10. We cannot drum up this life; we cannot achieve it by exhorting people to work harder, pray harder, and serve harder. In short, it can't be manufactured by human effort. It is only produced as we discover that wonderful rest known as abiding in Christ.

In that regard – it is better that we do nothing! Nothing but fix our eyes on Jesus the author and perfecter of our faith.

Even if it means taking a year off the busyness of church life - because at the end of that year we may be so full of the wonder of our salvation, that works of Life appear like fruit on a vine, all by themselves. *The branch's task is to simply abide, the vine does the real work.*

When I say it like that it is easier to picture the issue as it related at first to Adam and Eve - they decided to produce fruit from their own resources. That is what the Knowledge of Good & Evil is all about – producing life from our own resources.

That's why "God doesn't care what you do – but he cares a great deal that you gain a revelation of what Christ has done". Without an all-consuming revelation of Christ and Him crucified, we fall back to works produced from our own resources.

Paul said in 1 Corinthians 2:2 "For I resolved to know nothing while I was with you except Jesus Christ and Him crucified". And in Philippians 3:8 "What is more, I consider everything a loss because of the surpassing worth of knowing Christ Jesus my Lord, for whose sake I have lost all things. I consider them garbage, that I may gain Christ".

Paul didn't come with action plans, 6 steps to maturity, or church growth programs. He preached but one thing "Christ and Him crucified" – and this approach was sufficient to spread the gospel to the 4 corners of the world.

It is the same today, the Spirit of Christ cannot be systemized, he can only be grasped by revelation. It is a revelation that comes as we discover that Christ did so much. More than the payment of our sin penalty, and more than providing an example of a life well lived. He came to kill our post-Eden nature and re-birth us with his own; he came to bring us back to the garden of God.

This death is not merely a metaphor; it's the real death of our old godless nature that Paul refers to quite frequently in his letters. Galatians 2:20 "It is no longer I who live but Christ who lives in me" Colossians 3:3 "For you died and your life is now hidden with Christ in God".

Chapter 5. Flesh Deeds Spirit Deeds

Our Old Nature wants religion, it wants systemized Christianity, it wants a culture that gives us something to do – but it does not want to rest in the sufficiency of what Christ has done in giving us his nature.

The up-shot is that Christianity has developed a new kind of spirituality which has the appearance of real spiritual life, but in reality is simply the Old Nature dressed up in new clothes. This new kind of spirituality has an impressive language, it has heart-rending worship, and powerful preaching – but it remains a mere human copy of the real thing. The tragedy is that many follow the crowding masses, repeating the phrases of this new culture but having no real revelation of the cross of Christ. They believe that it is the real thing, when it is really no more than a well scripted copy.

Our only option is to stop following ministries, and discover Christ for ourselves!

I'm not advocating leaving your church or disconnecting yourself from the community of believers that is your home. But I am advocating that no church or fellowship of believers can take the place of your true spiritual home, Christ himself. Like Paul we must count all things as garbage compared to the surpassing worth of knowing Christ Jesus our Lord.

Then true fellowship can emerge, a fellowship that starts with Christ and expands outward by his Spirit.

It takes great courage to look away from the systemized institutions of Christianity for our source of Life. We are used to being fed by a sermon, a time of corporate worship or prayer, or perhaps the fellowship of believers. Only one thing can truly feed our hungry hearts, *the one who said feed on me!*

Chapter 6.
Feeding on Christ

This 'feeding on Christ' may for a time be a little isolating. Not because you have distanced yourself from anyone – but because nobody quite gets what you are on about.

That's ok, it's a journey that each of us must take alone. It's not like going to a conference with a car load of believers, all full of the expectations of the experience ahead.

> *This is more akin to a pilgrimage to the cross*
> *– you just go there and ask God to show you what it was all about.*
> *And then you go back, time and time again, all by yourself*
> *– and gradually the magnitude of it begins to dawn on you, and*
> *you stand amazed by it.*

Like the well-known hymn penned by Isaac Watts; "We must survey the wondrous cross on which the Prince of Glory died". As we read his magnificent hymn from start to finish, we get the impression that Isaac Watts was actually standing at the foot of the cross, stunned by what he saw. The result of such a survey is that the words of Jesus found in the book of John "You will come to him and receive life" will slowly overwhelm you. What had previously been mere theology will become your personal experience.

You might remember back in chapter one I made reference to my state of emptiness as a result of being stripped of my financial security, and the accumulated assets of a life's work in property development, during the Global Financial Crisis. It was a sense of having nothing left in my inner reserves, nothing

It was a foreign place for me because I had always been able to keep going and push through, I had always been able to dig deep and find a way. But not this time, I had reached the end of myself – the tenacity that had created my wealth and self-worth was exhausted.

I have since wondered if this emptiness is akin to the way Adam operated in the very beginning. Not because Adam came to the end of himself like me, but because it was his nature to relate to God as one empty of self-worth. He received the nourishment of his soul from Christ, not himself - *or his own goodness.* You could say that he was created empty of self-worth, because his God-worth filled him to overflowing. The emptiness I experienced positioned me for a revelation of the wonders of *Christ and Him crucified* that I had not previously grasped in my many years as a Christian. I believe it was because I had inadvertently stopped eating from the Tree of the Knowledge of Good & Evil, and was able see that an alternative existed - the Tree of Life.

Even though I was a genuine Christian man all my life; *elder, worship leader, preacher* – it wasn't until I was empty of self that I realized I had been dining at the table of self-made worthiness the whole time. I was not an egotist or a bragger, I was not narcistic or self-adulating, that's not what I am describing here. I was simply living my life the best way I knew how, according to the rules that had stood for ages.

Added to that, I had seriously confronted the validity of a form of Christianity that had failed me so dismally when I needed it most. I had tested the model handed to me by the culture we call Christianity, and found it sorely lacking.

And so my pilgrimage began. I began to search the scriptures for a better way, a different Christianity that was based on the same scriptures, but that

Chapter 6. Feeding on Christ

actually worked at a much deeper level. I read the word and I prayed, and I prayed and read the word – this went on, day after day, for about six months. It was at a time while my business was unraveling around me, I could do little but watch it happen so I had the time, and I spent countless hours in our church just searching for Jesus.

My search began with a quest to find out what I had missed – what I should be doing differently. I looked hard for any item that needed adjustment in my life, so that I could expect things to work out better in the future. Did I need to pray more, did I need to pray differently, maybe I should give above the tithe, should I extend my quiet times, maybe engage in a new ministry? Ultimately all these things were merely minor adjustments, I needed a major overhaul.

The breakthrough came as I was considering Hebrews 12:2 "Let us fix our eyes on Jesus, the author and perfecter of our faith". It dawned on me that I had been fixing my eyes on myself (what I should do), instead of resting in the work that Christ had already completed for me. It was a classic case of 'the Human Drama' at work – I was looking to myself as the solution, when all along Christ was waiting for me to draw life from him.

The trouble was: *I didn't actually know how to!*

I had been a part of the system my whole life but I didn't actually know how to draw life from Christ. Don't get me wrong, I had applied all the spiritual principles for my whole adult life. I had been involved in all the usual activities and spiritual exercises – but I didn't actually know how to rest with confidence in his word. I didn't know how to simply believe that my life was safe with him – all I knew how to do, was apply myself to the spiritual activities, that those more spiritual than me said I should.

The fact is: I had to learn to believe all by myself.

All around me were people involved in every conceivable Christian pursuit – but no one seemed to be actually, 'believing in Jesus'. There was plenty of religious language and rhetoric; there was no shortage of anecdotes and catch phrases about God. But scratch the surface, and no-one seemed to know how to take God at his word, and rest there. There always seemed to be one more spiritual task to perform, one more positive confession yet to attend to… *so that God would come through.*

As I fixed my eyes on Jesus I made a remarkable discovery – Jesus had already come through. He had come through when he dealt with sin on the cross, and he had come through when he had provided life for free in the garden.

He had never ceased from his 'life giving work' – *it was who he was and still is.*

I didn't need to do anything to get the breakthrough; I needed to simply believe that "because Christ was complete in every way, so was I". *Because I was in him and he was in me.*

This led me to the conclusion that there was nothing I needed to do to attract the full flood of God's favor, blessing, and love. My only task was to believe that he could actually be that good. It has brought real meaning to scriptures like Hebrews 4:10 "For anyone who enters God's rest also rests from their works" and also Jesus' statement in John 6:29 when asked "What must we do to do the works that God requires?" Jesus answered "The work of God is this; to believe in the one he has sent".

My old thinking had been so deeply ingrained in the ways of the 'Human Drama' that it took quite some time for the truth of these scriptures to gain real traction. All of my natural instincts reared up, *'It just couldn't be true, that would be an indulgence of the worst kind, it would be lazy and irresponsible'.*

But slowly my fear subsided, and I am at last at peace. Funny thing is that this peace has given me a new energy to speak of Jesus in a way that I have not previously known. I am beginning to understand the verse in John 7:38 "Whoever believes in me, as Scripture has said, rivers of living water will flow from within them."

Chapter 6. Feeding on Christ

Now I read a scripture like Hebrews 13:5 "Never will I leave you; never will I forsake you" – and I take him at his word. I am learning to rest, and I am learning that God can be trusted… *with everything!* After all these years I am at last learning to ease back into his loving goodness, instead of straining to maintain his favor. It is so much better this way.

It begs the question; how does one make the transition from straining to resting? How does one stop feeding on the 'wrong tree', when it is all you, and your church environment, has ever known? How does one step out of the 'human drama', and back into the garden?

This is perhaps the most important component of this book; it is the 'pearl of great price' – the very treasure of heaven. It is a subject that deserves very careful thought because its counterfeit 'religion' is always lurking, masquerading as the real thing – waiting to shift our gaze away from Christ and back onto ourselves.

Chapter 7.
The Pearl of Great Price

One of the subtleties of our post-Eden thinking is that we see ourselves as a 'work in progress'. We perceive ourselves as somewhere along the maturity scale – and that God has just a few more rough edges to round off, and we will be ok. We have a tendency to believe that the circumstances of life are God's tools for getting us into shape. We take the illustration of the potter's wheel and apply it to our daily lives, and conclude that God is busy at work shaping us into instruments of usefulness.

The circumstances of life may indeed shape us for the better, but I know of plenty of times where they have shaped someone for the worse.

The notion that a good God, causes bad things to happen to us
- to make us into good people,
is just the kind of bad theology that we can expect from the wrong tree.

In fact the opposite is true; Christ completed a wholesale change of our nature when he took our sin onto the cross. He became SIN for us – he became our sin nature, *mine and yours* – and in return gave us his own righteous nature. 2 Corinthians 5:21 says "God made him who had no sin to be sin for us, so that in him we might become the righteousness of God".

We are not in transition toward righteousness… *as we mature in our Christian walk.*

God would never leave us on such shaky ground as to place any hope in the very nature that caused the problem in the first place. God did something far more robust than depend on us to improve as we walk out our days on earth. On the contrary, he killed our old nature – it was morphed into Christ's work on the cross, and he took us home early.

John 5:24 says "Truly I say to you, whoever hears my word and believes him who sent me <u>has eternal life</u> and will not be judged, he <u>has</u> crossed over from death to life". It means that by simply believing we are rescued from satan's kingdom, and re-established in the garden of God, *in an instant.* We are home, it is done, and we are back where Adam started.

> ***All that remains is for the veil of nature to fall away when we die, and we will see with clarity that which has been ours all along.***

Time and time again I have heard Christians talk of the battle between our old & new nature – as if there is a tension that exists, and we must apply ourselves to the task of beating back the Old Nature by our good living. There is only one area that remains in tension, and it resides between our ears. We must renew our minds to understand with clarity the work that Christ completed, and we must enlighten our hearts to grasp the magnitude of our salvation.

> ***In short, we must begin to see ourselves as God does.***

As far as God is concerned we are 'hidden with Christ in God' - 'we are seated in heavenly places' - 'we are joint heirs with Christ'. This is how God views us because he is fully informed of the magnitude of Christ's achievements. All that remains is that we also see with his eyes… *and agree.*

Another hangover from our post-Eden thinking is our understanding of God's commands. In fact, the 'Human drama' is obsessed with God's commands – it is the currency of the Old Nature, because it loves doing.

Chapter 7. The Pearl of Great Price

Commandments in the context of our Old Nature are always associated with reward and punishment. They are associated with reward and punishment by man's choice not God's. God did not design the system; it was a system that man placed himself in to. The system that God designed *(if you can call it a system)* was altogether different - goodness and life flowed simply by being in union with God. It was automatic; it was based on the essence of who God is – He gives life, he gives virtue, he gives worth. He does this because it is his nature to do so. If he ceased to do it, or did it conditionally, then he would cease to be the God he claims to be.

We are no longer in the system that connects reward and punishment with commandments, so we need to know how God's way works, and get on-board with his mode of operation.

Jesus operated in the 'New Commandment' way. We read in the book of John 5:19-20, "Very truly I tell you, the Son can do nothing by himself; he can do only what he sees his Father doing, because whatever the Father does the Son also does. For the Father loves the Son and shows him all he does".

Jesus was in such a bond with his Father that he replicated his Father's heart on earth. He was able to do this because he was completely secure in the loving union they shared. He saw his Father's nature, and acted according to it, as if it was his own – *and indeed it was.* In effect, Jesus was empowered by what he saw in his Father, without it he was powerless.

Elsewhere in the book of John, Jesus refers to the New Commandment. This has always loomed in the mind of believers as the last-best, good work that we do for God. John 15:12 "My commandment is this; love each other as I have loved you" - yet, who can love as Jesus loved? This kind of love is impossible within the context of our old nature; we must grasp the union that Jesus opened up for us if we are to have any hope of loving in this way. We must love with the unforced rhythms of our new God-nature, resting in the completeness of that union, to love in this way. Then that love indeed flows forth from God's own heart, through us, to others. To do otherwise is to attempt to please God with the filthy rags of the flesh.

Could it really be possible to love in this way? Not only possible, it is the very work that Jesus undertook, *'the restoration of the temple'* - you might say. *And we are that temple, the very habitation of God.*

Our senses rebel against such talk. Our natural instincts are too well informed of our shortcomings to take literally our status as God's temple – the place inhabited by his holy presence. We look at our lives and see the weaknesses of our human condition and conclude that the writer is simply using a bit of literary license – *how could someone so perfect, dwell in someone whose life is such a train wreck?*

It is this apparent oxymoron that obscures perhaps the most sublime of all truths. In exactly the same way that Jesus was in his Father, so also we are in Jesus, and Jesus in is us! Jesus presence in the Father has no more to it, than our presence in him! Check out John 14:20 if you don't believe me.

> ***Jesus presence in the Father has no more to it, than our presence in him!***

Our five senses and our intellect are the servants of our Old Nature. Their role is to deliver information to us 24/7. They have been charged with the responsibility of declaring truth to our hearts ever since we split with God and had to work out our own reality. In the first place they were designed to provide simple earthbound facts; too hot, don't trip, smells funny, what was that noise, etc. They fed information to the intellect and the intellect made decisions based on it.

When man walked away from his union with God, the five senses and intellect were elevated to a status they were never intended for. They took over the role that was previously undertaken by the 'eyes of our heart' and began to deliver a flow of information that was dramatically inferior to that which came from our God-nature. Genesis 3:7 "Then the eyes of both of them were opened and they realized they were naked". It wasn't that they were previously unaware that they had no clothes on, but rather they had previously

Chapter 7. The Pearl of Great Price

been clothed in the virtue of Christ. Good and evil was a new way of perceiving things. As soon as they were stripped of their righteousness, they needed to cover their exposed lives.

Ever since that time, man has been trapped in a cycle of clothing himself with his own virtue to obscure his spiritual depravity. His Old Nature reminds him day after day that he is devoid of any inherent goodness, and so he must commit himself to a life of carving out a meaningful existence from his own efforts.

When we bring this 'Old Nature' thinking into the context of the gospel, we conclude that Christ saved us, but we must maintain our salvation with holy living. *But this would be the most miserable of all ways to live - knowing that at five minutes to 'midnight' we might commit the unpardonable sin and go directly to hell.*

All of this fear and doubt because we have tuned our ears in to the wrong information.

It's the very reason why Paul exhorted the churches to renew their minds and enlighten their hearts. It simply isn't possible to live above the fearful demands of life and religion, while we depend on our five senses and intellect as the filter through which truth must pass.

Is it really possible to see with the eyes of the heart again after having lived under the instruction of our senses and intellect for so long? Indeed it is! We must regain our spiritual vision to see a greater reality than the one perceived by our senses, we must dust off our spiritual glasses and begin to look afresh at truth as God sees it.

Then we will see a world that is completely foreign to our natural world. It is an eternal world where the mysterious truth that we have somehow been recreated as beings in perfect union with Christ, is normal. It is the reality of our eternal existence... *and it has already begun.*

These 4 things define our new condition:

1. The perfecting of our spirits is complete; we are as holy as God - *right now*.

2. The life of Christ flows through us, as we rest in his finished work on the cross.

3. We are in perfect union with Christ, he is our new nature.

4. We now have the capacity to see, and live, from the same reality that God does.

There are many who would say that this is true in theory, that it is an eternal truth that applies to us doctrinally – a kind of positional truth, but not a practical one. They would say it's good to know this information, but it has no real application in the physical reality of the world we live in.

I would say in response to that: *what if they are wrong?* What if there is a dimension to our human existence on planet earth that we as believers have been missing for millennia? A dimension that has been obscured by our natural inclination to see reality with the eyes of the flesh – not the eyes of the heart.

Imagine for instance the way Jesus perceived reality. He saw the reality that existed in the eternal realm and spoke it into the natural realm. It seems he saw no reason why others didn't do the same.

In Mark 4:37-41 "A furious squall came up, and the waves broke over the boat, so that it was nearly swamped. Jesus was in the stern, sleeping on a cushion. The disciples woke him and said to him, "Teacher, don't you care if we drown?" He got up, rebuked the wind and said to the waves, "Quiet! Be still!" Then the wind died down and it was completely calm. He said to his disciples, "Why are you so afraid? Do you still have no faith?" They were terrified and asked each other, "Who is this? Even the wind and the waves obey him!"

It seems that by now Jesus fully expected them to see what they had in them!

Chapter 7. The Pearl of Great Price

That anything he could do, they could do.

In Matthew 14:15-18 "As evening approached, the disciples came to him and said, "This is a remote place, and it's already getting late. Send the crowds away, so they can go to the villages and buy themselves some food." Jesus replied, "They do not need to go away. <u>You give them something to eat.</u>" "We have here only five loaves of bread and two fish," they answered. "Bring them here to me," he said.

Perhaps Jesus was testing them;

I think he was simply speaking the truth as he saw it; they had within them the ability to do as he did.

In John 19:10-11 "Do you refuse to speak to me?" Pilate said. "Don't you realize I have power either to free you or to crucify you?" Jesus answered; "<u>You would have no power over me if it were not given to you from above</u>".

This time Jesus turns his challenge toward Pilate, he knew where the power really lay. And he had no hesitation pointing it out to the very man who would sentence him to death.

In Philippians 1:22 even Paul seems to see the eternal realm clearly "If I am to go on living in the body, this will mean fruitful labor for me. <u>Yet what shall I choose?</u> I do not know!"

Could Paul be saying that the choice is his? That would be a remarkable view of reality indeed.

The point in all of these scriptures is that the ability for us to actually see with the eyes of the heart is buried deep within each of us.

We have latent within us, the ability to see as Christ did when he walked the earth.

Chapter 8.
Seeing and Knowing

EPHESIANS 1:17-23 "I keep asking that the God of our Lord Jesus Christ, the glorious Father, may give you the Spirit of <u>wisdom and revelation</u>, so that you may know him better. I pray that the <u>eyes</u> of your heart may be <u>enlightened</u> in order that you may <u>know</u> the hope to which he has called you, the riches of his glorious inheritance in his holy people, and his incomparably great power for us who believe. That power is the same as the mighty strength he exerted when he raised Christ from the dead and seated him at his right hand in the heavenly realms, far above all rule and authority, power and dominion, and every name that is invoked, not only in the present age but also in the one to come. And God placed all things under his feet and appointed him to be head over everything for the church, which is his body, the fullness of him who fills everything in every way."

We need to unpack this:

For starters; why didn't Paul pray that they would have a religious experience? Why did he not pray for their personal concerns? Why did he not pray that they would get into the ministry, or get more power?

He prayed that they would see and know – *that is all!* He prayed that God would give them a Spirit of wisdom and revelation (spiritual knowledge and sight). And he prayed that the eyes of their heart would be enlightened so that they would know – (again, spiritual sight and knowledge). Could it be that Paul understood that if they could see what they had, then they would realize they had everything already?

> *Or to put it another way;*
> *Paul didn't pray that they would have anything in particular,*
> *because he knew they already had everything*
> *– all he prayed was that they would see, and know, what they had.*

That is so contrary to the way we do Christianity today – we treat people as if they are spiritual paupers, we give them of our perceived wisdom or ministry, and send them away, only to have them return for more at some future time. We should be filling them with the knowledge of their fullness in Christ, so that they never need ministry again. We should be imitating Paul, as he imitated Christ – telling people of the vastness of their salvation, and teaching them how to rest in it.

There was a time when I wondered why the Lord made it so hard for us to discover the fullness of our salvation. It seemed that he had presented us with a cosmic riddle that we could never hope to crack. Now I understand that it is simply because we attempt to apprehend the 'mystery hidden for ages' through the eyes of the flesh. He is not making it hard at all – it's just that he can't reveal himself through the very system that was established by man to conceal him. He is ready and willing to reveal far more than we could hope or dream of, but only as we view him through the eyes of the heart. If we go to him doubting our worthiness, or alternatively bringing our best human works, we will feel like he is made of stone. But if we come to him full of confidence in his goodness expressed through Christ, then he will show us wonders beyond our wildest dreams.

This instinct to go to God clothed in our best good works in anticipation of some spiritual or physical reward is reinforced in pulpits around the world Sunday after Sunday. In effect it would be like walking up to the Tree of Life, while eating an apple from the Tree of the Knowledge of Good and Evil. It would be like expecting the Tree of Life to applaud our choice to draw sustenance from poisonous fruit – *it just doesn't make sense.*

Chapter 8. Seeing and Knowing

It comes down to believing the right thing –
we must know the truth to be free.

All satan can do is lie, it's all he's got left – he has no power over us since he was crushed at the cross of Christ. People fear that he is doing all manner of harm to them and their loved ones; that he is causing all sorts of havoc in the lives of God's people. *But he has been disarmed, he has been humiliated in front of all heaven – he is a laughing stock.* Yet he manages to get away with lying to God's people day-in day-out. He has perfected the art of fooling God's people into believing they are weak, sinful and guilty when the opposite is true – *we are giants, and we are con-joined to Christ.* We cannot be any greater than that!

I truly believe that if we could see "the riches of his glorious inheritance in his holy people, and his incomparably great power for us who believe" – then Christianity would be a whole new ball game. There is a scripture in 1 John 4:17 that deserves serious consideration; "because as He is, so also are we in this world". This scripture is saying that the way Jesus operated as a man, the way he was able to perceive his Father's presence and understand spiritual things, is the same way that we can. There is no difference between the operating system that Jesus used, and the one that we have – *it's been returned to us again, it's just that we don't see it.*

It is imperative that we get this sight functioning. Without it we are groping in the dark, but with it we are able to see our inheritance, and lead profoundly meaningful lives from that knowledge. Everything that is of value in this life flows from our wisdom and revelation of Christ. Proverbs 4:17 confirms this "The beginning of wisdom is this: Get wisdom. Though it cost all you have, get understanding".

This understanding is not a complicated matter; it's not that we must all become theologians or doctrinal scholars. We must simply gain a revelation of just this one thing "Christ and Him crucified". I don't need to understand all about how my car works (theology) - but I do need to confidently understand that when I stand on the brakes the car will stop.

Similarly with our understanding of Christ; we don't all need to be bible scholars, but it is impossible to place great confidence in something, if we don't understand the basics correctly. If we understand what he accomplished on the cross and who we are as a result, then we will confidently live lives of faith. We cannot work-up that faith on a case by case basis. We must gain such a confident understanding of who we are that faith is always on standby.

As the old hymn writer said "We must gain an interest in his blood". Unfortunately, most of us have an interest in the activities and culture of this big thing called Christianity, but very little interest in his blood. I don't mean that we are to have some macabre fascination in Christ's blood, but that we are to discern the magnitude of what took place when it was shed for us… and plunge in to its accomplishments with total abandon!

It's almost become old-fashioned to talk about the blood of Christ and his sacrifice for us. It seems we have progressed on to much more modern pursuits and causes. In fact, many folk find it down right uncomfortable and unsettling to bring up the subject. But the reality is, *it's all we've got.* 1 Corinthians 1:18 says; "For the message of the cross is foolishness to those who are perishing, but to us who are being saved it is the power of God" – *we must not let the cross also become foolishness to those who are being saved.*

If we are to 'see and know' the right information we must begin to look through the eyes of the heart, and understand with the mind of Christ. Unfortunately most of us approach the things of God with our Old Nature (the Human drama) as our filter, rather than our New Nature (the Life of Christ) as our filter.

The filter that we choose to use will determine whether we read words of life or words of death in the scriptures. Words of Life set us free, they draw us toward our righteousness in Christ, they lift all guilt and condemnation, and they fill us with a joyful anticipation. Words of death keep us bound up, they keep our focus on our weak human condition, our failings, and inadequacy's, and they diminish our expectations for the future.

Our Old Nature is wired-up to read only words of death in the scriptures – it is its operating system. The *Old Nature filter* through which all scripture must pass is this: "What do I have to do to activate these words, what is my part that enables the favor and blessing of God to manifest into my life". The Old Nature considers it risky and reckless to simply rest in the goodness of God, it always swings its gaze across to lifestyle, and religious activities, to find security and wellbeing.

The New Nature is wired-up to read only words of life in the scriptures – it is its operating system. The filter through which all scripture must pass is this: "What has Christ done to activate these words, who and what am I now that Christ has translated me into the Kingdom of God". The New Nature considers it natural and logical to rest in the goodness of God, it swings its gaze across to Christ and Him crucified, to find security and wellbeing.

To illustrate this let me give a real life example. I recently heard a Christian school teacher tell her pupil that God would be happy with her if she behaved properly. This sounds correct at first, but on further examination it is in fact *'words of death'* masquerading as spirituality. God is happy with the child because Christ has purchased the child's life and transferred her into the kingdom of God – *period!*

If the child fails to behave well next time she will instinctively think that God is not happy with her. The teacher is training the child to eat from the Tree of the Knowledge of Good and Evil, instead of the Tree of Life.

This little example epitomizes the thinking that pervades much of Christendom. We instinctively default to Old Nature thinking, yet somehow expect New Nature outcomes to result. Even Einstein said that the definition of insanity is "Doing the same thing over and over again, and expecting a different result".

All through the ages Christianity has taught people to think with the mind of the flesh, and expect the outcomes of the spirit

– *it hasn't worked; it's time we reprogrammed our minds!*

Chapter 9.
The Old Nature

Most Christians I know think of the Old Nature in terms of the behavior it produces. Their thoughts immediately go to listing sins committed; in particular the really bad ones like killing, stealing, committing adultery, lying, jealousy, gossip, etc. The result is that we view the sins committed as the problem, and not the nature that produced them. The logical conclusion of this thinking is that the Old Nature is relatively benign - as long as there are no apparent sins on display. Or to put it another way; the issue is whether we commit a sin, not whether we have a nature that may produce sin.

Our tendency to see our individual sins as the problem, rather than the inherent nature that produces those sins, has caused Christianity to miss the most important thing about our salvation. We have fixed our focus on Christ's work in paying the penalty for our sins, rather than his work in crucifying our Old Nature. Indeed his payment of the penalty is of great significance - but if that is all he did then we remain people who are constantly damaging our relationship with God when we sin, and having to repair that damage through frequent repentance.

To have our sins forgiven, but our Old Nature remain intact (or even in tension with our New Nature), is tantamount to leading such a guilt-ridden life that we are no better than the unbelievers. We are still stuck with the problem that we produce sin, perhaps even the same amount of sin that the unsaved produce.

It is this dilemma that produced religion in the first place (religion being the practice of activities intended to satisfy God). To have our sins forgiven by a benevolent God - only to sin again, requires a system that maintains our standing with God in some way. Religion is that system. In Old Testament day's man's right-standing with God was maintained by the various sacrifices, holy days and the priestly role. In our day it is maintained by ongoing repentance, confession, and a variety of religious and personal lifestyle habits.

The introduction of religion is a post Eden phenomenon. Religion is the servant of the Old Nature. Before man stepped away from his union with God there was no need for religion – it was a time when God was, and man was, and it wasn't necessary to wrap a system of behavior around a living truth.

This post-Eden system should have ended when Christ rose from the dead and returned us to the ways of the Garden. It should have ceased to exist much the same as a game of football ceases when the final whistle is blown. Yet, we continue to play a game that is over – running madly around a playing field as if it really mattered. When in reality, the game has been won by Christ, and he has invited us back to his place for the post-game party.

Don't confuse religion with Christianity.

Religion is the practice of religious activities to satisfy God. Christianity is the fellowship of believers already in perfect union with their loving God. These 2 are vastly different. They are the difference between playing a game for all your worth, and celebrating the victory at the after-party.

The notion that humankind are responsible for the ongoing maintenance and management of their salvation, after Christ has given it to them by grace - is the same as saying that our behavior at the after party has the potential to disqualify us for the victory that was sealed when the umpires final whistle blew. We became victors in that moment in time when the whistle was blown,

Chapter 9. The Old Nature

and we equally become saved in the moment in time when we receive Christ's victory on the cross.

The real question for us is this, "dare we believe that the love of God, and the finished work of Christ, can have achieved so much - and dare we cast ourselves with full abandon into the fidelity of it? Leaving behind our dependence on the good deeds of the flesh to provide our security".

We have come full circle; we are back at Jesus statement in John 6:29 "The work God requires is this, to believe in the one he has sent".

The problem for many Christians is that they don't see the incompatibility between believing, and the operating system of the 'human drama'. These two cannot exist harmoniously together; they are as incompatible as light and darkness. It is simply not possible to do the one thing that God requires "believe in the transformative power of Christ" - and continue to trust in our own good deeds to please God and retain his favor.

We cannot live in two kingdoms at once; we must choose to be citizens of one or the other.

When we view the 'sin' problem as a vast collection of wrong deeds, we end up trying to live in two kingdoms at once. We attempt to live in the Kingdom of God as his saved people - and also live by the rules of the kingdom of darkness, as we attempt to *hold on to* our place in the kingdom of God, by our right living.

The only way to resolve the matter is to understand that the Old Nature was crucified with Christ, along with all of the sinful deeds it produced. It is this understanding that gives full meaning to the term 'born again'. To be 'born again' requires that the Old Nature die. We cannot be 'Born of God' - John 1:13, and also children of the nature of the flesh.

To be 'born again' is not merely a modern Christian label, nor is it a status that has the afterlife as its objective. It is to undergo a change to the essence of our being to such an extent that we have become a brand new creature, never before seen on the planet since Adam and Eve.

As far as God is concerned, we do not exist apart from our union with Jesus.

Chapter 10.
The New Nature

In contrast to the Old Nature, the New Nature has very little focus on our behavior – not because it doesn't value right behavior, but because it knows that right behavior is simply the overflow of Living in the Spirit.

The Old Nature concerns itself with the appearance of spirituality through the conduct of an outwardly visible good life. The New Nature has no such concern because it is aware than any outwardly visible good behavior is worthless, unless it springs from the presence of Christ within. Accordingly these visible good deeds are not generated by the individual, but by the New Nature we have in Christ. They are the product of the New Nature – just as sin is the product of the Old Nature.

As such; walking in the Spirit is not measured by the good deeds in one's life - but by whether the person has grasped the wonder of Christ and Him crucified, and placed themself into that revelation. In the same way; walking in the flesh is not measured by the sin in one's life - but by whether the person has failed to identify themselves with Christ and Him crucified.

It is quite possible therefore, for a Christian to walk in the flesh in exactly the same way as an unbeliever. Being a believer doesn't automatically provide us with a Life in the Spirit; it may simply be that we have determined where we will spend eternity.

That is essentially what walking in the Spirit is, *'It is living in eternity early'*. John 5:24 says "I tell you the truth, whoever hears my word and believes him who sent me has eternal life and will not be condemned; he <u>has</u> crossed over from death to life". The New Nature recognizes this as a fact, and constructs a life accordingly.

The New Nature lives as Adam first did – he lived spiritually in God, and naturally on earth – (both at the same time). The New Nature is fully and deeply informed that God is its real home, and it spontaneously lives from the resources of God's kingdom. It does not timidly approach God for a morsel from the great banquet, but confidently takes its place with dignity and joy around the table of God's blessing and favor. The New Nature is a son not a servant, and the assets of the kingdom await his distribution.

If we live our lives from the operating system of the Old Nature we will always come to God based on the perceived merits of our life. If we live our lives from the operating system of the New Nature we will always come to God on the merits of Christ's life. It doesn't matter how spiritual our lives may appear, if that appearance is generated by guilt, obligation, or self-effort, it is no more than filthy rags.

The New Nature produces a life of faith *naturally*. It simply responds to the truth that it has perceived through the Word and the Spirit. It does not need to pump-up faith, or generate it by spiritual aerobics as the Old Nature does… *because the New Nature is deeply informed of the power of the cross of Christ.*

The Old Nature perceives truth through the five senses and the intellect; it then attempts to apply faith against life's circumstances to change them as required. The New Nature perceives a different truth based on the accomplishments of Christ; it then simply speaks this life out – it does not self-generate faith; rather it simply speaks out what it already sees and knows.

An example of this is found in Acts 3:6, Peter and John came upon a lame beggar, they did not pump-up faith to heal him, or go to God for a miracle, they simply gave him what they knew they had. But Peter said, "I do not possess silver and gold, but <u>what I do have</u> I give to you: In the name of Jesus Christ of Nazareth walk!"

Chapter 10. The New Nature

The new nature does not attempt to give something that it doesn't have, it can only give that which it is convinced is already in its possession
- as the dwelling place of Christ.

It may be that I am starting to sound like a stuck record – that I am repeating myself in a hundred different ways. To some extent that is true because this revelation changes everything – and everything proceeds from this one amazing revelation.

Let me put the revelation to you in a nut shell:

Before I believed in Christ I was a fully-fledged, ticket holding member of the kingdom of darkness – I just didn't know it. My nature was the same as the nature of satan – I had chosen through Adam to step away from my union with God and strike out on my own. I would be judged by my own juggling of the good v. evil equation, I would be god of my own life.

When I believed in Christ and Him crucified I was instantly translated into the kingdom of God – even though initially I couldn't really see it too well. My nature became the same as God's nature, righteous and holy in every way - this perfect nature is now the habitation of God with whom I am in perfect union. I no longer measure my life according to my deeds; I measure it according to the stunning victory Christ won for me on the cross.

My new status in Christ gives me the opportunity to live every day from the resources of heaven. It is the way I was designed in the first place. God's desire is to see me living so boldly, because it is perfectly in line with his own heart; he is good and he is love - *and he wants me to learn to count on it.*

Chapter 11.
The Big 10

Another thing that I grew up believing is that the 10 commandments were God's guidebook for my life. They were a written list that described his holiness, so that I could then construct a life that was compatible with his nature and expectations. A 10 point summary, what could be simpler than that? The heart of God spelt out in easy language so we could follow it, and achieve a good lifestyle. You could say that God gave the law to tutor us, so we could live right.

Once again my understanding of the 10 commandments was through the filter of an un-renewed mind, I had been applying the thought processes of the fallen nature to understand the matter.

To properly understand the point of the 10 commandments I needed to take a step back, and view their role within the bigger picture - I needed to understand them through the filter of the way things were before sin. I figured that if I could view them in the context of the Garden, then it would be reasonable to say that their application to me now, would be the same as their relevance to Adam before he lost his God-nature.

It's interesting that God planted the Tree of Life and the Tree of the knowledge of Good and Evil, in the center of the garden – Genesis 2:9. It shows that God held Adam and Eve's right to choose very highly, he would never control their will by hiding the Tree of the Knowledge of Good and Evil out the back.

He allowed them to compare the fruit, and decide for themselves how they would like to live their lives.

We need to understand that God's directive in verse 17 "You must not eat from it" was not a command like in the 10 commandments. It was more of a 'cause and affect' warning – much as we would warn a child not to cross a busy street. God did not give them one simple command as a test of their obedience; he simply warned them that consequences followed if they chose to be nourished by their own good v. evil living.

As it turned out the temptation was too great. Adam and Eve chose to be 'like God', knowing about good and evil, and as a consequence they lost their holy naivety. This was the warning that God had issued, if they chose the wrong fruit they would lose their naked innocence. It is interesting that the word 'sin' did not appear at this time. God did however articulate the results of their decision to understand good and evil – *ground was cursed, work for food, pain in childbirth etc.*

The word 'sin' doesn't appear until Genesis 4:7. Cain was angry and the Lord explained to Cain the way that the system of good v. evil worked – "If you do what is right, will you not be accepted? But if you do not do what is right, sin is crouching at the door; it desires to have you, but you must master it".

This is the first time in recorded history that the relationship between doing what is right / and acceptance, is spelt out so clearly. Sin is likened to a controlling master that must be overcome; right behavior opens the way for acceptance.

The contrast is striking;

pre-sin = the holy innocence of being created in the image of God – *(sin free)*.

post-sin = a wrestling match with sin to gain acceptance – *(sin conscious)*.

This 'sin free' existence which first defined Adam and Eve's life is the same 'sin free' existence that is again ours through faith in Jesus. Once again we are nourished by the Tree of Life, just as Adam and Eve were at the start. We have a holy innocence as our New Nature – as Paul says in 2 Corinthians 5:21, "God made him who had no sin to be sin for us, so that in him we might become the righteousness of God".

As such our relationship to sin has also changed. For Cain (and all of humanity that followed), sin was "crouching at the door, desiring to possess us". For us who rest in Christ, we have returned to our pre-sin status. Paul states this clearly in Romans 6:14, "For sin shall no longer be your master, because you are not under the law, but under grace".

Returning again to the 10 commandments (the law): The verse above says that we are no longer under the law but under grace – so what is the point of the 10 commandments for us today? Some would say that they remain a useful guidebook for life, a set of tracks that we travel on to keep going straight.

It begs the question; if sin is no longer our master, why do we need a guidebook? And if we decide to live without the guidebook of the law, where will we get our guidance from? This question is very helpful in clarifying the way forward for anyone who wishes to live according to their New Nature.

The Old Nature is locked in a mind-set of 'doing what is right to be accepted'. In contrast the new nature asks the question, 'now that I am accepted in Christ, how shall I live?' The answer is simply this 'you will live in the Spirit'. You will live as Jesus did, in restful assurance of the Fathers pleasure. Even before Jesus had commenced his earthly work, Matthew 3:17 describes the Father's heart; and a voice from heaven said, "This is my Son, whom I love; with him I am well pleased."

God's pleasure for Jesus existed outside of Jesus fulfillment of his earthly work. It was this pleasure that energized Jesus to complete his work on earth. The same can once again be said of us. God's pleasure in us is independent of our earthly deeds; this pleasure enables us to fly on the breath of his Spirit within us.

The contrast between the law and grace are clear; the law demands constant attention in an attempt to remain master of life and its challenges.

Grace flies above the constraints of the law
- it is carried aloft in the adventure of the Spirit,
energized by the pleasure of God.

Satan would have us keep our focus on the law – he doesn't want us to fly on the wings of God. If we fix our eyes on the Big Ten, we will miss the adventure of a lifetime. It is this Spirit flight that we were born for – it is our true nature and destiny.

Paul made the contrast clear as he explained the old and new covenants.

Chapter 12.
The Covenants

To a large extent the covenants have gone relatively un-noticed by the church. We know that they are there, but their significance seems to be more relevant to the nation of Israel, or to the Old Testament context - than to us in this day and age.

If we are to fully grasp the New Nature, then it is important that we understand the covenants.

The bible has many covenants contained within its pages. Covenants are agreements – some with conditions and some without. I want to explore in detail two covenants that God gave to man – the old covenant (also known as the Mosaic covenant), and the new covenant (ushered in by Jesus).

The old covenant was enacted by God when he gave the tablets of stone to Moses on Mount Sinai. It had as its backbone the 10 commandments, but also many other rules and regulations that governed sacrifices, worship, and life in general. It went like this; God told Moses to come up to Him and hear his words. Moses related these words to Israel as follows; "When Moses went and told the people all the Lord's words and laws they responded with one voice, everything the Lord has said we will do" - Exodus 24:3.

The question is this; why was it necessary for the Lord to give the law at this time? They had managed ok without the law for 1000 years already since the fall - or about 600 years since God promised to bless the world through Abraham's seed.

The law was given because they were about to enter the promised land – the promised land is a picture or shadow of the Kingdom of God, and they needed a priestly system to live within it. The priestly system was the intermediary between the people and God, it was to provide right standing for the people, or else they would be destroyed by God's holy presence among them.

The people were eager to enter the Promised Land and be under the protection and benefits of the Lord's presence, so they confidently agreed to the Lord's words and the Law.

At this point I need to clarify that although God enacted the Law and the Old Covenant, it was not by his design that such a system would be necessary. The Law became necessary because the people had been placed by Adam into a good v. evil performance-based existence. God never intended that they would be governed by their performance, but now that they were, he articulated very clearly what they would need to do to have his presence in their midst.

In other words, the need for the Ten Commandments came from man's initiative not God's. God simply provided the only way forward within the operating system _they_ had chosen.

The New Covenant was a completely different system (if you can call it a system) – it came into operation when Christ rose from the dead. In a nutshell Christ satisfied all of the expectations of the Old Covenant in one fell swoop, and then he proceeded to demolish the actual Old Covenant as well.

Getting back to the football analogy – you could say that Christ won the game, then purchased the franchise for the game, and then proceeded to destroy every remnant of the game, it's rules, its hierarchy, and its entire operations. The Old Covenant no longer exists, in fact; Colossians 2:14 puts it

Chapter 12. The Covenants

this way "Having canceled the charge of our legal indebtedness, which stood against us and condemned us; he has taken it away, nailing it to the cross". Christ nailed the Old Covenant system to the cross and destroyed it forever, and then Christ became our eternal high priest in its place.

This event is clearly outlined in Hebrews 8:6-11. It is a big chunk of scripture, but worth including in it's entirety for its overarching summary of the New Covenant.

"But in fact the ministry Jesus has received is as superior to theirs as the covenant of which he is mediator is superior to the old one, since the New Covenant is established on better promises. For if there had been nothing wrong with that first covenant, no place would have been sought for another. But God found fault with the people and said: "The days are coming, declares the Lord,
when I will make a New Covenant with the people of Israel and with the people of Judah. It will not be like the covenant I made with their ancestors when I took them by the hand to lead them out of Egypt, because they did not remain faithful to my covenant, and I turned away from them, declares the Lord. This is the covenant I will establish with the people of Israel after that time, declares the Lord. I will put my laws in their minds and write them on their hearts. I will be their God, and they will be my people. No longer will they teach their neighbor, or say to one another, 'Know the Lord,' because they will all know me, from the least of them to the greatest. For I will forgive their wickedness and will remember their sins no more. By calling this covenant "new," he has made the first one obsolete; and what is obsolete and outdated will soon disappear".

In summary of this wonderful passage of scripture - the covenant that God introduced on Mount Sinai became obsolete when Jesus established the New Covenant. This New Covenant can be summed up with these words: "They will all <u>know</u> me". It is a new operating system that is based on one thing 'knowing God'.

John 17:3 says "Now this is eternal life; that they may <u>know</u> you, the only true God, and Jesus Christ, whom you sent".

We <u>know</u> God, when we lose ourselves into the amazing revelation of Christ and Him crucified – *that's it!* We have ticked all the boxes, we have satisfied all of the requirements – we are home. *This is the New Covenant.*

> ***As I was saying earlier; the New Covenant is not a system, it is a person - his name is Jesus.***

Chapter 13. Why Are We Here?

Here are a few reasons I've heard:

- The reason God has placed us on this planet is that we might fulfill the great commission.

- God has a unique plan for every life that is revealed as we surrender ourselves to him.

- Christianity is a purpose-driven experience directed by the local church.

Paul makes a rather quirky statement in Galatians 5:1 "It was for freedom that Christ set us free". It sounds like he is repeating himself, until we examine it a bit closer. I believe that he is saying this; "Christ has set you free, now live free". The implication is that it is possible to be set free by Christ, but not actually live the life of a free person. It would be like being set free from jail, and then spending your time on the bench outside the jail. *That isn't living in freedom.*

In effect, Paul is saying: "The reason you are here is to be free".

The issue that Paul was addressing is circumcision; it was the last-best, good work in Paul's day. He was saying that Christ came to set us free from everything that religion requires of us – but I wonder if he was also saying something even more profound. Could it be that he was saying; "That Christ not only set us free from our obligation to religious behavior, but that he set us free from the nature whose existence was defined by its good v. evil behavior."

Now that would be freedom indeed, it would mean that we are released to have a fresh look at how we go about living our lives. In fact; it would mean that we can live life just as Adam and Eve did before the fall. So let's have a deeper look at how they lived back in the garden.

Firstly; in Genesis 1:29 we read that God said "I give you every seed-bearing plant on the face of the whole earth and every tree that has fruit with seed in it", then in Genesis 2:19 "Now the Lord God had formed out of the ground all the beasts of the field and all the birds of the air. He brought them to the man to see what he would name them: and whatever the man called each creature; that was its name" and finally in Genesis 2:25 "The man and his wife were both naked and they felt no shame".

The first scripture says that God provided for Adam and Eve all that they would need to live on, even more than that; he gave them every tree or plant on the entire planet - he lavished on them the entire produce of the earth. They were free of the responsibility to provide for their needs. Though they did indeed work in the garden – it was God who was their source.

The second scripture says that God allowed man to name every creature. This was more than simply giving them a suitable sounding word for their name, this was defining their existence. God allowed man to assign whatever characteristic he thought best, for every creature on the planet – he delegated the dominion of the earth to man. Adam was free to say, life on earth would be, as he determined it would be.

The third scripture says that Adam and Eve were oblivious to their nakedness. They had a nature of holy innocence; they had no concept at all of shame or guilt. This is not a statement limited to their lack of clothing; it goes to every aspect of their existence. They were free of any expectation to perform in any way. There were no rules, no rewards, and no process necessary to have God's favor. They had everything already.

I believe it was this complete lack of expectation, and total confidence that God was their source of everything, that allowed them to live a vitally fulfilling and giving existence. It was for freedom that they had been set free – and this freedom released them into a life in the Spirit.

Had God controlled their life in any way, or limited his favor and blessing to keep them on track – then they wouldn't have been free, and he wouldn't have been God. But God was true to his nature, and he set them free to live as they chose. He had put his nature within them, so they naturally lived as God did. It's the same way Jesus lived as expressed in John 5:19 "I tell you the truth, the Son can do nothing by himself; he can only do what he sees his Father doing".

It's not that Jesus was under the control of his Father. But rather, that Jesus and the Father had exactly the same nature – and Jesus spontaneously did whatever the Father did. Not that Jesus copied his Father on earth, as his Father mimicked some miracle up in heaven - but that the heart-beat of Jesus for humanity was exactly the same as his Father's. If Jesus chose not to do whatever he saw his Father doing, then he would be denying his nature, and he would cease to be himself. This true-to-self characteristic of God is expressed in 2 Timothy 2:13 "If we are faithless, he remains faithful, for he cannot disown himself".

And that's exactly what happened with Adam and Eve, they chose to act outside their God-born nature with the result that they ceased to be who they were. They disowned themselves and became people who had a self-born nature all of their own.

But now we have a God-born nature once again. The reason why we are here is to live wonderfully free lives true to that nature - it's called living in the Spirit. It's not something we have to try and do; it just flows out of us as we rest in the lavish bounty of God's love and kindness. Paul expressed this for us so beautifully in 1 Corinthians 3:22-23 "all things belong to you, and you belong to Christ; and Christ belongs to God".

Adam and Eve didn't have to try to be true to their nature - while they rested in the kindness and goodness of God it was as natural to them as breathing. It took a deliberate act of separating themselves from God, for their God-nature to die.

Again; this is the sentiment expressed in Hebrews 8 that we looked at in the last chapter; "No longer will they teach their neighbor, or say to one another, 'Know the Lord,' because they will all know me, from the least of them to the greatest".

> *This 'knowing the Lord' is not an intellectual thing*
> *– it is the knowledge that comes from having the same nature*
> *as God, not learned - but <u>in-born</u>.*

You might be thinking; "what about Christians who don't live according to their new nature?" In fact, they too 'know God' – but that knowledge is clouded by the habits of the old nature. In other words; their old nature is dead, they just don't realize it.

Every born-again person has a new nature. Sadly for many, the system that the Old Nature created to please God still has a hold on their thinking, and so they live as one would live that hasn't grasped the New Nature through the renewing of their mind.

This New Nature is our inheritance, it is the children's bread, the gift that Christ came to give – we really should grasp it with both hands, *don't you think?*

Chapter 14. Letting Go

Twenty first century Christianity is very fad oriented. It's quite normal for Christians these days to latch on to the teaching of the latest guru, only to head in the opposite direction a month later because we had a visiting ministry that said so.

Such statements as; 'What is the Lord doing in your midst?' or 'What is the new thing God is teaching you?' are the language of modern Christianity.

This didn't seem to be the case in the early church. Paul's statement in 1 Corinthians 2:2 "For I decided to know nothing while I was with you except Jesus Christ and Him crucified" would be out of step in today's contemporary Christian circles. We would never dream of settling for yesterday's revelation, we are always looking for the next, the new, and the latest.

We are fad junkies!

We need to stop looking for God to do 'a new thing', and discover up-close and personally the only thing that he has ever done – reveal Christ and Him crucified. In John 15:26 Jesus says, "When the Counselor comes, whom I will send to you from the Father, the Spirit of truth who goes out from the Father, <u>he will testify about me</u>".

The one thing that God is doing these days
is revealing to Christians the stunning accomplishments of the cross of Christ.

This fetish for the 'next thing' causes modern day Christians to be always looking at the horizon, always waiting for God to move, always anticipating his presence and power. In keeps us future focused as we await God's touch, or his next move in our lives. Yet that is not the message of the gospel. The gospel message is now, not in the future – it is in our possession today, not the hope of tomorrow.

This future focused Christianity keeps us from our inheritance, because it anticipates an action of God yet to come. It is fixed on a thing that God has yet to do or complete - for us to truly possess the kingdom. It's a lie that keeps us milling around the activities of the culture we call Christianity, instead of stepping into our Christ-given inheritance today.

In this book I have already made a few statements that some might consider extreme or scandalous, here is another; "God is not doing anything! He is finished doing what he does, he has completed his list of activities – he is done!"

Let me explain. When Christ declared on the cross "it is finished" before he sighed his final breath, he meant the task that he had come to fulfill was finished - he had achieved his goal. Humankind was rescued, life had been breathed back into the lost, and we had been carried back into eternity. Christ has re-established us back into the garden of God where we began – *he had done his job.*

He does not have any further installments up his sleeve – we have everything, we have been made new. We have the kingdom in it's entirety, there is not a single thing that God has yet to do for humanity… *but to continue revealing to them what is already theirs.*

You might be thinking; 'What about healings, provision and other miracles?' - All of these are already ours as we learn to rest in the sufficiency of Christ's work. Remember that scripture in 1 Corinthians 3:22-23 "all things belong to you, and you belong to Christ; and Christ belongs to God" or another one like it in 2 Peter 1:3 "His divine power has given us everything we need for

Chapter 14. Letting Go

<u>life and godliness</u>". We are fully loaded, God-born new creations, re-made in the image of God, with the whole banquet of heaven resident within us.

What about this one; Romans 5:17 "For if by one man's offense death reigned by one; much more they which receive abundance of grace and of the gift of righteousness shall <u>reign in life</u>", or perhaps this one in Ephesians 1:3 "Praise be to the God and Father of our Lord Jesus Christ, who has blessed us in the heavenly realms with <u>every spiritual blessing</u> in Christ."

We are present tense people, not future tense. All things belong to us! We have everything we need for life and godliness! We are reigning in life! We have every spiritual blessing!

Perhaps you are thinking; "that's all very well in principle, but my life is still in need of God's touch today". Our circumstances and troubles cause us to seek God's involvement in our lives – they are a very apparent and demanding fact that can't be ignored, or resolved with spiritual platitudes. In short; *"they are real!"*

I do not wish to diminish the need of any person or the seriousness of their circumstances. What I have to say next is intended to bring relief, not further difficulty. My desire is to see people lifted up not crushed by more demands and expectations.

I agree that our circumstances are real, that is not in question here. What is in question is this; "Did Christ resolve them on the cross when he returned us to your rightful place in God's kingdom, or is God still administering the benefits of his kingdom to us day by day, in accordance with our requests, and his will?"

In my view we can't have it both ways; we are either fully 'in Christ' or not at all. We cannot be partially in Christ. And if we are fully in Christ, then we have everything we need for life and godliness. This is not some sort of teaspoon administration of God's blessings and favor, it is life in abundance.

So if we have everything we need for life and godliness – where is it? *I'm glad you asked.*

One of the reoccurring themes of this book is 'seeing and knowing' – this simple truth unlocks the kingdom of God within us. Take for example 'God's presence'; it is something most Christians hunger for, they want God's hand to be deeply touching their lives. When we read Hebrews 13:5 we find God saying "Never will I leave you, never will I forsake you" – if this scripture is true then why do we continue to seek God's presence?

> *Perhaps it is because we measure God's presence*
> *by our feelings and not by his word; and if so,*
> *perhaps we should get on with life in full assurance*
> *that his presence is always ours.*

If we can see with the eyes of our heart, and know with the renewed mind, that God is always with us; then we do not need to seek him any longer – he has been found, and we are in him, lost in his presence forever.

This confidence in God's word is what I will call 'letting go' – it is a practice that is completely foreign to our Old Nature. Our natural response is to retain control and push through, it is to dig deep and call on our inner resilience. This natural response obstructs the superior way of resting in the goodness of God – *believe me, I know, I've been there.*

It is akin to taking a leap into the darkness – all we have is Jesus word, "come to me all you that labor and are heavy laden and I will give you rest". Will we take the leap? Will we let go of all the props we have set up around ourselves? Or will we hang on grimly to our control… *and ask God to help if he wouldn't mind?*

The old adage "God helps those who help themselves" is not actually in God's word, it is a fabrication of those who won't abandon themselves into Christ's ability to hold us.

Chapter 14. Letting Go

This thinking holds Christians around the world trapped in the system of the Old Nature - God can either be trusted with everything, or he can't be trusted with anything. He has either fully resolved the plight of humanity, or he has resolved nothing. He is not a God of half measures, if he was, he would be just a man like us – he is infinite, he is perfect, and he gets the job done.

Why would we not completely trust and let ourselves go into a God like that? *Because we don't actually see and know that he is like that.* Sure we may have learned all the Christian responses, we may have familiarized ourselves with the clichés and catch words of Christianity - <u>but that is not the same as examining the cross of Christ and declaring to yourself once and for all, that it was enough.</u>

A fascinating exchange takes place in John 12:28-30 Jesus said, "Father, glorify your name! Then a voice came from heaven, 'I have glorified it, and will glorify it again'. The crowd that was there and heard it said it had thundered; others said an angel had spoken to him. Jesus said; this voice was for <u>your benefit</u> not mine". Jesus was showing us how it is done, he was saying; "I don't need the comfort of God's touch upon my senses, I have resolved in my heart long ago that he can be trusted – but for you who are still walking according to the senses, this voice is for you."

We are no longer walking according to the senses as the people in Jesus day were. Christ has died and risen, he has crucified our Old Nature with him – we have been born again of God. Our senses are not an accurate measure of truth, only a revelation of Christ and Him crucified can truly be trusted for that.

There is a way to live that is so superior to the old way of the 'human drama' as to render it foolish. It requires that we gain a deep revelation of Christ and cast ourselves fully into the fidelity of that revelation. There is no other way – we can't let God into some rooms of our life, but not others. If he can be trusted with anything, he can be trusted with everything – and if we only entrust a part to him, then we are effectively entrusting nothing to him.

As for our earthly troubles; they are real – but Christ is the greater reality. If we rest in his presence within us, then these earthly troubles are hidden in his mighty, life-giving, work on the cross. Our part is to simply rest in the notion that our salvation could actually be that good. We take the needs of life to him, and leave them at the cross - *he can handle anything...*

Chapter 15.
How to Receive

THE first and most important aspect of receiving anything from God is to 'see and know' that you already have everything. Without the confidence that we are truly complete in him *(in spite of the loud voice of our circumstances)* we might as well beg God as the pagans do when the going gets tough. The difference between us and the un-saved is that we are people of faith, not of sight.

This confidence in God is not like its worldly counterpart – positive thinking. It is not some sort of mind game that we employ to get ourselves into a positive frame of mind. It has nothing to do with visualizing our goal, or positive self-talk, or the other mantras of the new-age crowd. This confidence is about determining in our heart once and for all, that God is, and does he what says - and casting our entire existence into that fact. It is putting all our eggs in his basket, and burning the bridge behind us – *to combine a few useful clichés.*

There can be no half measures, it is not a thing done lightly. It is not a formula or method – like the power of praise, or positive confession - *it is a person,* his name is Jesus, and he wants us to believe that he loves us more than our wildest imaginations. He wants us to leap out of all our worldly props and securities, and land in him.

Colossians 3:4 puts it beautifully "When Christ, who is your life, appears..." Paul had taken the leap, Christ was his life. Christ was not just the cause he served, or the passion of his heart – Christ was actually his life.

As far as God was concerned, Paul and Christ were inseparably joined,
(Paul did not exist apart from his union with Christ)
– and Paul was simply agreeing with how God saw things.

In the modern world we have become accustomed to 'receiving from God' through a person who is suitably gifted to deliver God's touch to us. We stand in prayer lines, we listen to u-tube teaching, we engage in prayer circles, and we soak-up words from the big-shot ministries. But we are not particularly good at simply resting in the accomplishments of Christ.

It is this 'intermediary, or middle-man thinking' that has made the most natural of Christian benefits into the most elusive. Our union is with Christ, he is our real spiritual self – yet we go to a person or ministry to obtain the benefits of this union. It just doesn't make sense. Christ died to make his home in us, he brought with him his entire kingdom – yet we don't know how to directly partake of this amazing fact without the help of another Christian… *that has no more than we have.*

The presence and kingdom of Christ is no more real in the visiting ministry, or great preacher, than it is in us. When will we lift our eyes off earthly intermediaries and rest in the abundance of our union with Christ? When will we take the leap and settle in our hearts that Christ is enough – even for me?

Perhaps the reason we doubt that the vitality of Christ within us is equal to his presence in others, is that we are painfully mindful of our human weaknesses and failures. We cannot imagine that our capacity to receive from God is no different to that of people with front-line ministries - *because they appear spiritual, and we consider ourselves un-spiritual.*

John 3:34 says "for God gives the Spirit without limit" and in Acts 10:34 "I most certainly understand now that God is not one to show partiality". There is no difference between me and you, and the biggest names in ministry on the world stage – *other than 'seeing and knowing'.*

Perhaps we should also add to this that the sort of confidence involved doesn't happen overnight. We don't gain this revelation easily because our senses fight tooth-and-nail against it. Many give up, frustrated that God seems to hide himself from the masses, and only reveal himself to the big shots. But we must not give up, *for this is the pearl of great price.* We must not rest until our Old Nature lies in our wake, and the adventure of the spirit beckons us to new horizons.

I have spent much of this chapter speaking of the reality of 'Christ in us' rather than 'Receiving from God'. I have done this deliberately because we cannot receive from God apart from a deep revelation of the scale of the salvation Christ gave us. Sure we may get an occasional touch or tingle from the ministry of another person – but this should not be compared to the scale of the fullness of Christ that is latent within us.

It is this 'giant within' that must fill our screen, not the circumstance or need that presses against us.

To that end; our need to receive help with our many problems and troubles, must become secondary to our need to gain a clear view of the vastness of our salvation. Our circumstances will yield to the blood of Christ, but first we must loose ourselves into the truth of it - such is the stunning power that is contained within his work in saving us.

> **This power awaits but one catalyst to release it into our lives;
> that we see and know 'Christ and Him crucified' in all his
> glory and wonder...** *and believe.*

For many this doesn't seem like enough, it seems painfully idle and lacking real intent. In reality the opposite is true; it is the difference between the meager activities of man, and the same power of God that raised Christ from the dead.

We see this in practice in such incidents as found in Acts 28:3&5 "Paul gathered a pile of brushwood and, as he put it on the fire, a viper, driven out by the heat, fastened itself on his hand… But Paul shook the snake off into the fire and suffered no ill effects". Paul went on preaching as if nothing had happened – and this confidence caused the poison of the viper to yield to the blood of Jesus.

He was able to do this because he had a clear view of his status 'in Christ' - it was the primary truth that filled his screen. He did not have to pump it up, or press-in for it. It was a simple fact that was more real to him than any other thing – as far as Paul was concerned; "Christ had him, more than the viper had him".

In much the same way we must lay hold of the revelation that we are 'in Christ' to a far greater degree than we are in our circumstances. It is this revelation that will cause our troubles to flee from the presence of his glory; they must flee because they are the product of a fallen world that has been overtaken by the kingdom of God.

The process of renewing our mind in this way takes time. The Holy Spirit will enlighten the eyes of our heart day by day, layer upon layer, precept on precept – our part is to fix our eyes on Jesus the author and perfecter of our faith. We cannot hurry the process much as we might like to, because we have much to unlearn and relearn. Maybe that's what Jesus was referring to in Matthew 7:14; "But small is the gate and narrow the road that leads to life, and only a few find it".

Paul stated his view of earthly difficulties quite clearly in Romans 8:18; "I consider that our present sufferings are not worth comparing with the glory that will be revealed in us". He had that far-off look in his eyes, he could see his eternal home – and the buffeting of life couldn't hurt him. A similar sentiment is expressed in Hebrews 13:6; "So we say with confidence, the Lord is my helper; I will not be afraid. What can man do to me?"

Please understand that I do not wish to diminish the gravity of the circumstances that press against us, or the anguish they bring. But our faith in Christ cannot hope to transcend these troubles if we wallow in the shallows.

Chapter 15. How to Receive

We must grow strong in our conviction of Christ's presence, so that, like Martin Luther we declare in the face of great oppression "Here I stand, I can do no other, so help me God. Amen".

Christ's death and resurrection broke open the floodgates of Gods favor into our lives, our circumstances will declare to the contrary – one will bow the knee to the other, according to the perspective we choose to have.

Jesus said in John 16:33, "I have told you these things, so that in me you may have peace. In this world you will have trouble. But take heart! I have overcome the world."

Dare we take heart, and take him at his word!

Dare we stare-down our troubles… knowing that Christ is all, and in all.

Chapter 16.
The Body of Christ

THE title of this chapter evokes some sort of emotion in most Christians. They may be happily settled into their local community of believers, and feel a great sense of warmth when the term 'Body of Christ' is used. They may on the other hand have bitter recollections of pain or control that they suffered in the church and the term may cause them to shudder.

The Old Nature and the New Nature have very differing perspectives when it comes to the church.

The Old Nature views the church as an organization of people that meets in a building on Sundays, and relates to God through a system of worship and fellowship. It finds comfort in this mindset, and prefers to be contained within well-constructed rules and protocols. The Old Nature relates to God primarily through the various activities of this local group of believers. The Old Nature finds purpose and meaning within the church.

The New Nature is quite different in its view. It has grown confident in the continual presence of the Lord, both within, and outside, of the organizations activities. The New Nature highly values fellowship with other believers, but relates to God just as confidently when not in the company of other Christians. The New Nature does not need a system of rules and protocols to function; it rests in the ability of the Spirit of God within, to provide direction. The New Nature finds freedom and life in its union with Jesus - and brings these into the fellowship of believers.

> *The practicing of religion is the invention of the Old Nature.*
> *The freedom of Life in the Spirit is the essence of the New Nature.*

Over the centuries the church has attempted to blend the two, but it can't be done – they are opposites. That's not to say that the church is a failed experiment, or that the regular gathering of believers is a waste of time – not at all! There is much to be valued in the fellowshipping of one to another as Paul exhorts.

But it is necessary that we know where to go - *to get what!*

Only a deep and personal walk with Christ can carry us above the storms of life. Only an independent grasp of the magnificence of Christ and his salvation, has the ability to truly satisfy the thirsty soul of humanity. This deep revelation is not to be found in the activities of the collective body of believers, it is found at the foot of the cross where we discover our dear Savior. In short; the church is not our Savior, Christ is.

The fellowship of believers is where this deep revelation can be lived out as we share, encourage and bless each other in the mutual building up of the body of Christ. The church should be a place where believers are constantly reminding each other of the wonder of the cross of Jesus, so that our security rests squarely on his shoulders, rather than those of our brothers and sisters.

The Body of Christ is much bigger than the institution of the church. It is an invisible union of every saved person who ever lived on the planet. It has no boundaries, neither race, nor denomination, nor worldly status. It has no leader but the Spirit of Jesus its head, and it has no membership or formal affiliation. This body is located in heaven; the members of this body live for a time on planet earth, but for an eternity in their union with Jesus. This body is sometimes known as the Bride of Christ, the New Jerusalem, or the Universal Church.

While we remain in our earth suits we live in this body by faith in Jesus. It is by his grace alone that we have been joined to this amazing, Spirit directed,

Chapter 16. The Body of Christ

holy and righteous union. We bring nothing to it, yet we gain everything from it.

When we die, and the veil of the flesh falls away, we will discover what we have had all along. We will see with clarity that we have been made like Christ. His great riches, glorious inheritance, incomparably great power will be clearly seen – and we will know that we are the fullness of him, who fills everything in every way.

It is this understanding of the eternal Body of Christ that we have the joy of sharing with the fellowship of believers on the earth. This revelation gives meaning and perspective to our involvement in the earthly gathering of the saved, and our loving friendships with those not yet saved.

Chapter 17.
Beyond Grace

THERE is no doubt that the subject of God's grace is sweeping across all Christendom. It has become the most preached about, and written about, doctrine of Christianity in the last decade, if not longer. It is releasing those who have been held captive by legalism for their whole life, many breathing the fresh air of God's unconditional kindness for the first time ever.

Grace can be summed-up this way: <u>G</u>od's <u>R</u>iches <u>A</u>t <u>C</u>hrist's <u>E</u>xpense.

The grace revolution is changing the church as it lifts the heavy burden of obligation from the believer, and replaces it with the light yolk of Jesus. There is a collective sigh of relief, as people the world over are discovering anew the freedom of the gospel.

Grace removes the price tag from God's favor and blessing, it provides for free, that which the Old Nature had to pay for with religious activity. It lifts the lid off God's heart for humanity, and gives us access to his lavish kindness and mercy. No wonder it is gaining so much popularity across the globe.

But grace is not the end;
it is the doorway into the adventure of Life in the Spirit.

Many mill around the doorway, admiring its amazing goodness, stunned by the generosity with which it blesses and lifts up the weary soul. Many are so preoccupied with the dramatic change that grace has brought them that they fail to pass through the doorway – you could say they remain marooned in Graceland.

Grace makes no demands, it delivers no condemnation, and it exercises no control. Yet an adventure beyond grace beckons us to come, it calls to us to abandon our self-based lives and be carried by the winds of the Spirit.

It beckons us to walk through the door of grace into the heart of Christ and to surrender every fiber of our being into him - his kindness, his future, his nature. It beckons us to let go, and trust that he is able to hold the next second, the next day, the next year, and the next decade. It beckons us to believe that he is as good as he says he is – and he knows how to make our life into a beautifully crafted work of the Spirit.

Grace lifts the obligation of the law from us and it sets us free from the pressure of the 'Human Drama', but most of all - it positions us to enter into Life in the Spirit. We enter into life in the Spirit through the doorway of grace, there is no alternative entrance labeled 'Christian service', or 'good deeds' – there is but one way in, *through grace.*

As I mentioned earlier; sadly many don't progress through – and the reason; because they are so preoccupied with the fruits of grace, that they don't venture further into the life beyond.

Grace has opened up a new kind of prosperity teaching that declares 'you can have it all'
– but 'having it all' is not really the point of grace – Christ is.

Grace is about entering into a life that is so far beyond material & physical blessing, that they appear to be crumbs from the table by comparison. Grace is about entering in to Jesus himself; sure he brings the kingdom with him,

Chapter 17. Beyond Grace

and sure he has laid out a lavish banquet – but make no mistake 'He is the prize'.

You might be wondering; 'is there really a dimension to my Christianity that I have been missing? Is there really something dramatically more, that I have yet to enter in to?'

Indeed there is, otherwise why would Paul pray his Ephesian's 1 prayer? He prays that the glorious Father may give you the Spirit of wisdom and revelation, so that you may know him better. The Ephesians were clearly saved and living a Christian lifestyle – yet Paul identified that they needed more wisdom & revelation. They didn't need more of God, but they did need to see and know more clearly, that which was already in their possession.

Like the Ephesians we all need to know what we've got. It is this knowledge that releases us into verse 19 of Ephesians chapter 1 - *his incomparably great power for us who believe.*

It would seem that this power is more than having the ability to do supernatural acts; it is to live your entire life from a source other than the resources of the realm of nature. The old nature chose to separate from God and find its source of life within the natural realm, the new nature feeds on the life of Christ in the supernatural realm.

This may sound a bit fluffy and unrealistic. Surely the natural realm is where our existence is based and consequently where our source of life is to be found - to suggest otherwise would mean that we are not earthlings but some kind of alien beings.

We are indeed aliens and strangers in the world, as Peter describes us in 1 Peter 2:11. We are people who have passed through the cross of Christ and been changed so completely that we bear little resemblance to our old state - *we are not what we once were.* We were once people who carved an existence out of the good & evil we produced, and now we have been transformed into a people who are filled to overflowing with the righteousness of God.

This new being, indeed this new creation, lives from the life of Christ (it feeds on Christ) – we are therefore supernatural beings. We are no longer based in the realm of nature; we have a new home called heaven.

The reality of this transformation becomes fully expressed in our lives when we step through the doorway of grace and into our new identity in Christ. How do we take this step? – by believing all that the Spirit of wisdom and revelation declares to us about Jesus. Not simply a mental accent that he is as he claims. But that we leave behind our old life that looked for security in ourselves, and begin a new life that leans on Christ for our entire sense of identity – *Jesus called it feeding on him.*

It is this surrender to the revelation of Christ's goodness that is the beginning of a supernatural life. It is the beginning of living life as he lived life. All his security was drawn from his Father's love and acceptance, just as ours is drawn from Jesus love and acceptance of us.

1 John 3:2 says, "Beloved, now we are children of God, and what we will be has not yet been revealed. ... We know that when He appears, we will be like Him because we shall see him as he is."

When we see Jesus as he is, we shall be like him – *this is a truly wonderful scripture.* It speaks of his appearance at his triumphant return to earth. Yet it seems to suggest more than that because we have already crossed over from death to life - *we are already eternal beings.*

Could it be that we begin the transformation early if we see him as he is, *now?* Could it be that we become people of the supernatural realm as we take the step through the doorway of grace into Christ?

I believe this is exactly what it means. Christ is eternal, he has made us eternal – as far as he is concerned we are already fully fledged supernatural beings. All that awaits is that we see who we are for ourselves, and discover that he has made us like himself.

Chapter 17. Beyond Grace

The implications of 'seeing and knowing' are far reaching. To contemplate that we are actually not the being that we thought we were, is a real stretch. Yet this is the very thing Christ came to do, inject us with so much heavenly adrenaline that we cease to be 'of the earth' and to return us to our true eternal home, with him in the garden of God.

Ephesians 1:4 says that "we were *in him*' before the creation of the world" As far as God was concerned his eternal mind had already conceived us. Even though we were not yet in the flesh, we were already in the heart of God. This spiritual status is our real identity – it is our eternal condition, and it is who we are right now - in spite of the contrary evidence observed by our senses.

Grace is the doorway; it provides free entry into our new identity – we make this entry through faith.

> *We see it is true, we know it is real, we believe it - and step in.*

This spiritual sight and knowledge is rare these days. It seems to have been lost in the clutter of the culture and activities of church life, but I wonder if it was so rare back in the early church. Hebrews chapter 11 outlines a long list of those who exercised faith in opposition to the physical evidence reported to them by their senses and intellect. Verse 27 says something quite extraordinary "He saw him who is invisible". We cannot see invisible things with our natural eyes, only the eyes of the heart have that ability.

2 Corinthians 4:18 takes it a step further "So we fix our eyes not on what is seen, but on what is unseen. For what is seen is temporary, but what is unseen is eternal".

The things that are visible are merely the passing parade of our fallen age. The unseen realities are no less real for being invisible – and for us who have crossed over into eternity, they are the present day truth of our lives.

Grace on its own has the potential to hold us in the visible. It opens up such wonderful possibilities in this natural life that were previously not possible, that we are inclined to fix our focus here. But our real life lies beyond the doorway of grace, in the invisible realm of the kingdom of God – it is here that the adventure of the Spirit awaits our choice to enter.

Chapter 18.
To See The Invisible

THE wonderful story in 2 Kings 6:16-17 is familiar to many of us; "Don't be afraid," the prophet answered, "Those who are with us are more than those who are with them." And Elisha prayed, "O Lord, open his eyes so he may see." Then the Lord opened the servant's eyes, and he looked and saw the hills full of horses, and chariots of fire, all around Elisha.

The servant's eyes were opened to see that which was invisible to his natural eye sight. He had a short term glimpse into the realm that Elisha saw as normal. Elisha was a prophet; this supernatural sight was his every day perspective – he was able to view the natural realm / within the supernatural realm.

The supernatural realm (or heavenly realm) was the greater reality; the natural realm (or temporal realm) was hung in front of it - much as we might hang a picture on the wall. Elisha could see both, and this sight gave him confidence to live a supernatural life.

The Old Nature cannot see the supernatural realm;
it can only be viewed by the New Nature, as one hidden in Christ himself.

In the Old Testament this spiritual sight was limited to the prophets of God. We however are New Testament people. Our spiritual eyes have been re-opened by Jesus - *but they barely function as they should, through lack of use.*

It is up to us to let light into our spiritual eyes by embarking on the journey of faith. We must dial-down the information broadcast into our minds 24/7 by our five senses, and dial-up the information broadcast by the Word and the Spirit. We must dare to believe (truly and deeply) the extraordinary claim of Christ, that he has made his home in us.

As we begin this journey an interesting phenomenon begins to take place – the eyes of our heart slowly begin to work again. At first it is like the flash of a camera shutter - we know something just registered in our heart, but it came and went before we could hold it. Then gradually, week by week, and month by month, we begin to grasp our new identity in greater and greater clarity. It slowly takes over our screen and becomes our greater reality.

Our new identity begins to captivate our thoughts - to quoin a phrase "it becomes our magnificent obsession". Smith Wigglesworth would say "that he lived in heaven, on earth", and ever so gradually we begin to see what he meant. The realm of nature seems to diminish in its capacity to hold us, as we lose ourselves into the revelation of Christ and Him crucified.

A beautiful transformation comes over us as we realize we were born to live this way. Peace seems nearer, and blessing seems to be drawn to us as we rest from striving. It is the righteous heart of Christ continually attracting his Father's favor. His favor does indeed follow us, but Jesus himself truly is the prize – he possesses us, and we possess him, in the best possible way.

Ultimately we grow so deeply connected to Jesus that the things of the earth actually do grow strangely dim, in the light of his glory and grace.

This union with Jesus that gradually fills us more and more causes his mind to overtake ours. Such scriptures as 1 Corinthians 2:16 "But we have the mind of Christ"- had always seemed to be laced with poetic license and having little practical reality. But now I see such truth in these words as the vastness of his salvation takes hold of me.

Not that there is any inherent quality in me, *or any of us,* to attract such an elevated status; it is all from Christ, and his flood of goodness and mercy. Ego

Chapter 18. To See The Invisible

and self-promotion diminishes as Jesus comes clearer into view, such is the splendor of his glorious nature. Peter in Acts 10:26, Paul & Barnabas in Acts 14:15, and even the Angel of the Lord in Revelation 19:10, were horrified at the thought of drawing praise toward themselves. Such was their understanding of the stunning quality of Christ's holiness.

It is one of the great paradoxes of our faith that we have been elevated to such greatness through our union with Christ, yet we contribute nothing toward it. This stands so clearly in contrast to the world at large, and even some parts of the church, where big personalities are applauded, and even, *dare I say* worshipped. There are no super stars in heaven but God; we are mere men and women who have been filled to overflowing with Christ… *for free*.

In fact, I would say that any person, who draws attention to themselves, or their ministry, has not fully grasped the magnificence and unsearchable glory of Jesus. To see Jesus as he truly is brings us to our knees. It causes such a flow of genuine humility to come forth that we would never deem to bathe in his glory.

> *We are seated with him in heavenly places,*
> *yet we are struck with awe in his presence*
> *– such is the paradoxical life of one who has seen the invisible.*

There is no comparison for such an unreasonable notion in the natural world environments of business, wealth, beauty and talent. Jesus turns everything upside-down (or perhaps right-side-up). The first shall be last, the meek will inherit the earth, the sinner went away justified – he is master of the oxymoron and the contradiction, as he explains the Kingdom of God.

It is this contradiction that gives great hope to the vast number of people who have become disenchanted with religion, but deep in their heart retain a hunger for Jesus. They will be filled! It is the children's bread that they find the desire of their hearts, even in the face of having despaired with religion.

I myself was empty, and he filled me. He filled me with his invisible self, and the trinkets of life have lost their appeal in his glorious glow. I can't go back, I am ruined for self-based religion – *it is dead to me* – yet day by day the wonder of his presence fills me to overflowing, all because I asked him to show me Jesus… *and he did.*

Chapter 19.
Who Can Come?

There is a remarkable invitation in the last few verses of the bible. Revelation 22:17 says, "The Spirit and the bride say, 'Come!' And let him who hears say, 'Come!' Whoever is thirsty, let him come; and whoever wishes, let him take the free gift of the water of life."

Who can come? – Whoever is thirsty, and whoever wishes!

Who is making the invitation? – The Spirit, the bride, and whoever hears.

I always understood that the Spirit was calling us to come; but it was news to me that the bride was calling us to come, and a complete surprise that whoever hears can also call us to come.

Such is the invitation of God; such is the fullness of our salvation, that we have joined the great congregation of Jesus and together we call all humanity to come. Even in that first moment when we hear the call ourselves, we are joined to the joyful throng in calling the world to come. Such is his longing toward mankind – *it is the cry of the ancient garden resonating through the ages to all humanity,* "Come, lay aside your self-made life, and quench your thirsty soul on the water of life".

Who are we coming to? Certainly not religion; nor even the cause of the helpless or needy, not even the local community of believers – *we are coming to Jesus!* He calls himself the bright Morning Star, the Way, the Truth, and the Life. He is glorious beyond our wildest imaginings, and yet he knows our names and has written them in his book with his own blood – *we are coming to Jesus!* He is the mystery hidden for ages and now revealed to us. He is the Alpha and the Omega, the beginning and the end. He makes everything new – *we are coming home to Jesus!*

Hebrews 1:3-4, "The Son is the radiance of God's glory and the exact representation of his being, sustaining all things by his powerful word. After he had provided purification for sins, he sat down at the right hand of the Majesty in heaven. So he became as much superior to the angels as the name he has inherited is superior to theirs." *This radiant one is the object and destination of our hearts.*

Hebrews 12:22-24, "But you have come to Mount Zion, to the city of the living God, the heavenly Jerusalem. You have come to thousands upon thousands of angels in joyful assembly, to the church of the firstborn, whose names are written in heaven… to the spirits of the righteous made perfect, to Jesus the mediator of a new covenant". *It thrills the heart and fills us with such anticipation.*

The call to 'come' is so much more than its old covenant counterpart repentance. This call contains repentance *(a change of direction)* within it, but without the accompanying old covenant demands of deep sorrow, anguish, and determination to do better. These demands were the means used by our old nature to re-establish God's favor; they were the flesh agreeing to yield control. But they were a short term fix, the passing of time proved they had no real capacity to provide a lasting solution.

Jesus resolved that by crucifying our flesh with himself on the cross. Along with the passing of the flesh went the Old Covenant-style repentance that depended on man's changed behavior and attitude for its ability to please God. Our Old Nature had no lasting capacity to bridge the gap with God, so Jesus killed it once and for all – and in return gave us his own perfect nature.

Chapter 19. Who Can Come?

You could say that Jesus became our repentance, he satisfied every requirement of the Old Covenant, and then he destroyed that covenant forever.

The Old Covenant command to repent in sackcloth and ashes has been replaced with the New Covenant invitation to come. Every obstacle that depended on our Old Nature for satisfaction has been removed in one fell swoop by the death and resurrection of Christ – all that remains is that we come.

To come we simply leave behind our old self-dependent life, and come to Christ for life. It is not complex, nor does it have to be drawn-out; it happens in the twinkling of an eye. We step from the kingdom of darkness into the kingdom of light in the instant we see Jesus and say, Yes!

Jesus has no boxes we must tick to qualify, he has ticked them all – we just come because we are thirsty for his Life. Religion has a list of steps, processes and qualifications, it prescribes a series of hurdles we must jump to make ourselves ready; Colossians 2:14 tells us that Jesus nailed them all to the cross – *clearing the way for us to just come!*

It is yet another example of how wrong it is to bring the thinking of the Old Nature, and apply it to the free gift of life of the New Nature. The Old Nature cannot comprehend the workings of the New Nature; it is staggered by the notion that there are no strings attached. So it has carefully crafted a counterfeit, it mixes Christ's free gift with our most noble religious response, but it just doesn't cut it.

> ***Jesus put no obstacle in front of the weary soul – he just said come.***

Dare we believe that his love and kindness could be so generous; it would be a kind of love that is alien to this world of ours, it simply doesn't compute. The gospel of Jesus is never going to make sense to the 'human drama', 1 Corinthians 1:18 says, "For the message of the cross is foolishness to those who are perishing, but to us who are being saved it is the power of God."

Back in the Garden Again

If the gospel of Jesus makes sense, if you can rationalize it, or reason it out into the kind of thinking that fits into the common sense of this world – then it is probably not the gospel. The gospel of Jesus is outrageous, it's scandalous, it defies logic – *we get the kingdom of God for free, just by coming.*

The invitation goes out to the worst of sinners, thieves, prostitutes, liars, whoever – "come" my banquet is laid out, come and enjoy the kingdom prepared for you since the beginning of time.

This is the gospel I want, and it's the gospel I have - I can't go back, I am ruined for religion forever.

This is the gospel Jesus wrote in his own blood when he destroyed the old man-made way, it is the gospel the world needs now more than ever. Any person on this globe we call earth has the right to be a child of God; there are no exceptions or qualifications, no limits. He has reconciled this world to himself, he has removed the barrier of the flesh - now humankind can simply come to him.

Chapter 20.
Eternity

THE Old Nature has produced all manner of notions about eternity that pander to the desires of the flesh. The Old Nature wants heaven to be an extension of the earth, the next step that includes all of the characteristic longings and emotions that defined our existence here - *but which are in fact merely earth-based yearnings.*

The Old Nature perceives the next life as an improved continuation of life here - a life that is notable for our earthly relationships, and values our earthly lifestyle. Among these are such notions as family reunions, and get-togethers with those who departed before us, and perhaps conversations with Jesus about how well we did while on the earth, and how proud of us he is. Then we might take our place in the celestial choir and sing songs of praise for a few thousand years.

The New Nature knows different.

The New Nature is happy to be done with the pursuits of the 'human drama' and get on with an eternity hidden with Christ in God, Colossians 3:3. It won't be distracted from the union that it had lost for millennia, the union that defined its existence all those years ago in the garden of God.

It's not that the New Nature doesn't value the blessing of our deepest human relationships; it's just they pale into insignificance compared to the wonder and glory of our 'knowing and being known' by God. John 17:3 says, "Now this is eternal life; that they may know you, the only true God, and Jesus Christ, whom you sent."

Eternal life is not introducing yourself to Moses and giving him a pat on the back, or David and congratulating him on his sling shot accuracy. These matters will barely rate when we see Jesus face to face, and find that we really were re-made in the image of God by his blood.

If we empty all of these earth-based notions of eternity out of our minds, what do we have left?

Firstly Holiness; we have no earthly comparison to true Godly holiness. We are used to judging our worth according to where we sit on the scale of good and evil. Holiness is not what you do, it is who you are, and our God is supremely and unsearchably holy, He is the great "I AM" (not 'I do'.) Entering into God's holiness will blow away all of our earthly protocols – we will fall on our faces in stunned awe, yet paradoxically we will walk boldly up to the throne of glory as Christ does.

Secondly glory; again, we have no earthly comparison for divine glory. Such earthly concepts as fame, beauty, popularity and celebrity share no direct comparison with Gods glory. God is not at all like the earthly model / only expanded way out to infinity. His glory is his shining nature, not his best deeds or outward appearance. Our human nature revels in its own achievements; God's nature is quite different. It does not need to achieve anything to be validated, he simply is – and his achievements flow forth from that. In Exodus 33:18, "Then Moses said; 'Now show me your glory'. And the Lord said, 'I will cause all my goodness to pass in front of you, and I will proclaim my name, 'The Lord', in your presence". God's glory is not so much a physically visible thing; instead it is his goodness and his great name. A name is a word that identifies a person, not what they do. Names are mere labels in the earthly context - God's name is different, it is his astounding, blazing glory, we have no way of grasping the depth or even the true meaning of his name – but in eternity we will know.

Chapter 20. Eternity

Finally love; and again, we have no earthly comparison for God's love. Divine love is not an emotion, nor is it even an action – it is more akin to the value that God places upon us because we are his eternal possession, and because we are a part of his own being. God is love – he does not do love, he is love. This love radiates continually from him to us; he does not 'choose' to express it, because it is continually expressed by his nature. When we see this love as it truly is after we pass through the veil of death, we will never want to be without it again. It will fill our consciousness to overflowing; we will feed on it and be satisfied far beyond any earthly love previously known. This love will draw us to him like a magnet, it will be like an attraction never before experienced, and it will take hold of us and hold us forever in its intimacy.

To express the unsearchable holiness, glory and love which will be our home when we close our eyes in death, is way beyond our most lavish and extreme superlatives. We have neither the language nor understanding to express the inexpressible substance of God adequately. Paul used terms like 'immeasurable' and 'unsearchable' for good reason. The minute we attempt to contain God within the scope of human reasoning or language, we understate one thousand fold his wonder and majesty.

The Old Nature attempts to fit God into an earthly box (only bigger), it attempts to constrain eternity into scale, activities, duration and human experience. God is not in there. Even eternity, heaven, and all of creation are contained in him (not around him) – he is more than our minds can conjure, he is all and in-all.

I say all of this for a reason; to stretch our thinking beyond the safe boundaries of neatly packaged theology, and credible Christian concepts – he is incredible beyond our wildest imagination, yet he has made his home in our hearts.

Chapter 21.
Christ in Me

In Ephesians 3 and Colossians 1 Paul speaks of a mystery that has been hidden for ages. The mystery is 'Christ in you'.

Before considering the mystery itself; let's ponder why it has been hidden for ages. Surely God would not conceal a mystery of such importance from his beloved people for thousands of years. Surely he wouldn't play games of hide and seek just to test us.

It seems to me that the concealing of this mystery was caused by the flesh (not by God) - when humanity stepped away from its union with God. It couldn't be found because it is only known through the spirit. Man had effectively cut-off the revelation of 'Christ in me' since he left the Garden of God, because he had chosen physical sight over spiritual sight.

The mystery was hidden for ages - which means there was a time before it was hidden when it could be plainly seen. This mystery was no mystery to Adam and Eve; they reveled in it as the stuff of their daily existence – 'Christ in me' was as normal as breathing.

This mystery which was once known, then concealed for millennia, has now been unveiled to us again.

Christ has come back into the hearts of men. He never planned to be away for so long, he didn't want to be absent. But he couldn't make his home within the same environment as the 'kingdom of darkness'. His solution was to crucify the rebellious heart of man that harbored this environment, so he could come back home - bringing with him his kingdom of Life and Righteousness.

'Christ in me' is not a symbolic term used to describe an 'in principle' truth. It is not that his message, or his example, or even his mission, has somehow made itself resident in our hearts – it is that the actual person has moved back in.

How can one person live inside another? It defies reason to take such a thing literally, the implications would be staggering – it would mean that I have the fullness of God living in me.

If this were so it would explain a few things. It would explain how Adam was capable of defining the character and make-up of the entire animal kingdom, it would explain how Adam had the entire human race contained within his seed, and it would also explain how he could have considered himself to be like a god.

Jesus himself used the same term in John 10:34 "Jesus answered them, is it not written in your own law, 'I have said you are gods'." Clearly he was not saying that human beings are the Most High God of heaven, but he was acknowledging our inherent capacity to be the dwelling place of God. God never hid the amazing status that he had designed for us - he just never intended that we would walk away from our union, and attempt to be god without his indwelling presence.

This 'Christ in me' status is God's original design; and now it is our new divine nature that Peter refers to in 2 Peter 1:4. There is nothing presumptuous in our grasping of this new status as we rest wholly in the work of Christ; in fact it is what we were born for. The presumption comes when we assume this status apart from Christ and attempt the works of God without his indwelling righteousness as our powerhouse. That would be no different to the original problem in the garden, mankind assuming godliness - apart from his union with God.

As with all of the benefits of the kingdom of God, 'Christ in me' comes for free. The Old Nature doesn't like getting things for free from God, so it attempts to 'value add' by bringing along its own virtuous life. This is post-Eden thinking. 'Christ in me' is an all or nothing transaction – we either accept it for free on its original terms, or we live without it, and its outworking through us.

This is foreign to us; we are not naturally good at living boldly without bringing some human virtue to support that boldness. That is where believing comes in; it is the scandalous notion that we can live a life full of Christ, without contributing anything more to it than a deeply considered, but simple nod to him.

All it takes is belief that he is who he says, and saying, 'Yes, I'm in'.

It is the flesh-based instinct to position ourselves for God's presence through an acceptable lifestyle, which has obscured the mystery for so long. It was hidden from view by our own 'right living' - it is at last revealed again by our 'right believing'. Right living does not give us access to Christ, only right believing has that ability. It is the only work God requires, as expressed so clearly by Jesus in John 6:29 "The work of God is this, to believe in the one he has sent".

'Christ in me' is the game changer. Nothing can ever be the same after the vitality of the 'Spirit of Christ within' takes the steering wheel. It begins to feel so right that we wonder how we ever managed as Christians before. We are back in the operating system of the garden, and we can't go back for anyone's religious reasons.

Like Paul said in Galatians 2, "I no longer live, but Christ lives in me. The life I live in the body, I live by faith in the Son of God". This experience wasn't limited to Paul because of his mission or position; it is the reality that awaits every Christian. Paul had let go, he had crossed a line, and he no longer lived as before. 'Christ in me' had taken him over. We can let go just as Paul did, the same life of 'Christ within' awaits us.

It is not in God's hands but ours.
He has flung the door of grace wide open to us,
all that remains is that we walk through into the life we were born for.

Chapter 22.
Empty That We May Be Filled

No one wants to be empty. It is a forlorn and miserable place – there is too much hopelessness there, too much longing. We don't generally choose emptiness, it is thrust upon us – it's not normally a circumstance we seek out.

Matthew 5:6 says "Blessed are those who hunger and thirst for righteousness, for they will be filled". I have recently come to a new understanding of this scripture – those who hunger and thirst for righteousness <u>don't have any</u>, otherwise they wouldn't hunger and thirst for it. They will be filled because they are empty of righteousness, and they know it.

I have been empty, and I have been filled up. In my case; I couldn't be filled up, until I was empty.

I didn't deliberately live my life filled within the ways of the 'Human Drama'. I just did what everyone else was doing – I lived my life from the resources I had within. It wasn't until I ran out of internal resources that my emptiness surfaced, and I became ripe to be filled.

> **I wish I was empty sooner.** *But it's not something you do*
> *- it flies in the face of all we are told.*

Paul was full before he saw the blinding light on the road to Damascus, the blinding light emptied him of himself, and he became ripe to be filled by

Christ. He was full of his mission, his learning, his position, his status. It all emptied out when he realized his life was constructed on a self-made foundation based on the thinking of the system. When he was emptied and then refilled he finally grasped just how devoid of life he had been. Such is the contrast between being filled with self - and filled with Christ.

Paul's intentions had been noble and good, he was doing exactly what the system said he should, he was a rising star, the man to be watched – he was *full* of promise. But it wasn't enough. He needed an encounter with Christ, and he got one. It emptied out all of the previous fullness, so that Christ could fill him up with the real thing - himself.

It is interesting that Paul became blind. He needed to lose his natural sight so that he could see him who is invisible. When he received back his sight he was also filled with the Holy Spirit. Paul received more than his natural sight back - the eyes of his heart were enlightened too.

Desperation is indeed fertile ground for the Spirit of God to plant revelation in to. The hard surface of self-confidence has been broken up and prepared, for God to plant the seeds of life. I sometimes wonder if we need such an experience of broken-ness, to be open to the revelation of Christ and Him crucified.

In the end it comes down to this one thing: Christ cannot fellowship with darkness, he isn't satisfied to give a top-up of himself, into a vessel that has been feeding at the other tree. But he will fill up anyone who chooses to feed on him alone.

Is it necessary to be crushed by life to discover the mystery of Christ? I don't think so – it is simply necessary that we come to him devoid of the other things that compete to fill our screen. We don't have to become poor, helpless or broken… *just empty*.

There are many things that clamor to fill us. They are not all bad; in fact, many are very good and noble. Yet they have the capacity to obscure the

Chapter 22. Empty That We May Be Filled

wonder of Christ from view. Perhaps that is the hardest part of all – we have to empty ourselves of the good, so we can be filled with the best. The reason for this is that our Old Nature is so determined to find its security in what we do, not in what Christ has done.

It is hard to imagine that such good things as; fellowship, charitable service, religious piety, have the potential to obstruct our view of Christ – yet it happens when they become our primary focus.

Only Christ can have our heart, only he can truly satisfy.

Do we have to give these up? Not at all - but we have to grasp that they are the overflow of the revelation of Christ and not the means of obtaining it. In 1 Corinthians 13 Paul lists an impressive list of Christian endeavors and activities, he compared them to a clanging gong without love. That love is only found at the foot of the cross - it cannot be generated from within, it only comes as we view the cross of Christ and are stunned speechless by the spectacle which is Jesus. How sad to spend a lifetime engaged in the activities of Christian service, only to realize at the end of it all that it was just a lot of man-made noise.

In Philippians 3:8 Paul makes this remarkable statement, "What is more, I consider everything a loss compared to the surpassing greatness of knowing Christ Jesus my Lord, for whose sake I have lost all things. I consider them rubbish that I may gain Christ". In some translations the word 'rubbish' is exchanged for 'sewerage waste'. Paul considers every human endeavor to be sewerage when compared to the surpassing greatness of knowing Christ. In fact he goes even further than that; he cannot gain Christ <u>unless</u> he considers them rubbish.

Can we do both - (see Christ and serve him)? Eventually yes we can. But initially we must "survey the wondrous cross on which the Prince of Glory died, that our richest gain will turn to loss, and pour contempt on all our pride". There is no shortcut, no alternative route - the Spirit calls us to come devoid of all that holds us (both good & bad) – let's come.

Another hymn writer wrote these words; "Nothing in my hands I bring, simply to thy cross I cling". Many will attempt to do both - they will bring their best Christian lifestyle, *and ask Jesus to fill them too.* They will go away sad and frustrated, wondering why Jesus wouldn't fill them. He couldn't - they were already full. Yet if we say to Jesus "I have nothing in myself", no shred of self-worth, I am running on empty – then he will fill us and we will never be thirsty again.

Conclusion

I have written this book from my own experience, but it is not a book about me; it is a book about Jesus.

If it were a book about me then it would be reasonable for the reader to take my words and apply them to their life, much as we might apply a diet plan, or an investment scheme. It would be as simple as taking these words, and applying the formula.

But there is no six step plan, no system to follow, or program to enroll in – there is only Jesus. He is a person who lives in our hearts. He is not an operating system like 'Windows 10' that we can upgrade to, so that we can function better. And Christianity is not a religious system or organization - it is the most intimate relationship imaginable.

There are many who have grown tired of the operating system, they have lost their way as Christians, and put it all in the too-hard basket. The walking-wounded have vowed to avoid the church for the rest of their days, yet they still hear the gentle voice of the Spirit calling them to come.

If this is you; then this book is my attempt to say that Jesus wants you back. He wants you to consider the possibility that he really is all he claims to be, he wants you to come to the cross and have a life of such peaceful abundance as you have never before dreamed possible. He doesn't ask you to clothe yourself in religious garb – he just wants you to come.

There are others who have stayed faithfully within the church community. They may be busy in church life but there is a hunger for more. The years of service, and involvement in the many causes of Christianity have left them unsatisfied, they long for a deeper walk with Jesus but don't know how to find it.

If this is you; then I would say 'there is more' - be encouraged for he calls you to come also. He calls you who are weary and heavy laden to come and receive his rest. He doesn't care who you are; leader, or the one who sits quietly week after week in the Sunday service. He doesn't care how important or invisible you are in the scheme of church life; he just wants you to know that it's all about him... and to come.

And there are yet others who have never met Jesus at all, and have no intention of making his acquaintance because of the foolishness they see in religion. They find the ways of Christians a little amusing and puzzling, and the repeated party lines empty and tiring.

If this is you; be assured Jesus can be found today. He can come in to your heart in the twinkling of an eye and change you forever. He doesn't require anything of you but to believe that he could love you more than you love yourself, and all your days are safe in his care.

The road to the cross of Christ is not a busy highway – it doesn't hold the attention of the crowd like the endeavors of the world do. It doesn't make wild claims that appeal to the 'Human Drama'. It is travelled by lone pilgrims who have sold everything to gain the pearl of great price. They travel empty of self, yet full of joy for the wonder that lies ahead.

As they crest the last hill, their energy rises up and they begin to run, they can't help it for they have found the prize - Jesus himself. He is so pleased they have come, so very pleased. He paid such a high price that they might come.

His love shines like the sun, his life radiates forth like the heat of a summer's day, and his glory fills everything, like an atmosphere of blazing joy that goes on forever – and they run, *and they leap...*

Conclusion

They leap onto a cross that crucifies their pain and guilt and sadness, and they rise up clean.

Cleaner than clean, and whiter than snow - and they look for Jesus and find he is no longer there as before. He has been joined to them in Spirit and they have become hidden - more than that lost; lost in his goodness and love.

This goodness and love is the Garden of God, they have come home – forever.

www.ingramcontent.com/pod-product-compliance
Lightning Source LLC
Chambersburg PA
CBHW070629300426
44113CB00010B/1708